Praise for *Your Journey to a Prayerful Life*

"This book is masterfully written by a woman of prayer who learns it, lives it, and loves it. With each page turned you are invited into the presence of God, the one who listens, the one who responds, the one who loves. This resource equips, empowers, and calls people into a loving relationship with God almighty. It is comprehensive, instructive, inspiring, and rooted in the foundation of God's Word. I strongly recommend it for individual or group use. It calls people not only to pray but to live a life of prayer. The church will be deeply blessed by this study."

Kirsty DePree, Coordinator of Discipleship,
Reformed Church in America

"Prayer is a journey with God. Barb Schutt's love of prayer is the basis of her wonderful resource *Your Journey to a Prayerful Life,* which encompasses all aspects of growing in prayer. This is a great learning tool for the person who is beginning in prayer or has been praying for many years. Anyone can glean from these teachings. For each lesson, there are good questions to ask yourself, prayer suggestions, and action that can be taken for the reader to expand on his or her prayer life. Each week there is a memory verse that enhances each teaching. I highly recommend this valuable prayer tool to anyone who desires to deepen the journey of prayer."

Kathy Bruins, coauthor of *The Acts of Grace*

Your Journey
to a
Prayerful Life

*This study is dedicated to my daughters
Kara and Kendra,
who bring me joy as I see them mature
in faith and life.*

Your Journey
to a
Prayerful Life

BARBARA SCHUTT

CHALICE
PRESS
ST. LOUIS, MISSOURI

Cover photo: Alex L. Fradkin /Photodisc/ GettyImages
Cover and interior design: Elizabeth Wright

Visit Chalice Press on the World Wide Web at
www.chalicepress.com

10 9 8 7 6 5 4 3 2 1   09 10 11 12 13 14

EPUB ISBN 978-08272-44207 • EPDF ISBN 978-08272-44214

Library of Congress Cataloging–in–Publication Data

Schutt, Barbara.
 Your journey to a prayerful life / Barb Schutt.
  p. cm.
 ISBN 978-0-8272-4415-3
 1. Prayer–Christianity–Textbooks. I. Title.

BV215.S38 2009
248.3'2–dc22

                                                    2009024087

Printed in the United States of America

Contents

Acknowledgments

This book would not be in print without the prompting of the Holy Spirit and the encouragement of many people.

Many thanks to you, Dave, for being my primary cheerleader throughout this lengthy process.

Thank you, Mom and Dad, for teaching me to pray when I was a little girl.

I have appreciated the teachings and writings of many, but offer special thanks to Richard Foster, Jill Briscoe, Cynthia Heald, Jennifer Kennedy Dean, Cheryl Sacks, and Daniel Henderson for influencing my personal prayer journey.

Thank you to Steve Brooks, Jonathan Brownson, Kirsty De Pree, and my friends from the RCA Houses of Prayer Equipping Team. You kept the vision and passion for this project alive!

Special thanks to my prayer partners, Prayer Action Team, and Women's Bible Study Groups from Christ Community Church, Carmichael, California, who supported me in prayer and gave positive feedback along this journey.

I offer heartfelt thanks to Jeannette Post and Beverly Stroebel, my mentors and prayer partners in the writing process, and to my editorial assistant Kathy Bruins, for their encouragement, advice, assistance, and prayer support.

Also special thanks to Gay Reese for believing in my life and work enough to recommend that I submit the manuscript to Chalice Press.

You are all a blessing in my life. May God be glorified!

Foreword

Several years ago, I directed a four-year, national study of evangelism.[1] After interviewing 1200 people, conducting surveys, visiting churches, and analyzing mounds of statistics from churches in seven mainline denominations, we made a major discovery. *Prayer is the invisible underpinning of the great evangelistic churches.* We also discovered Barb Schutt!

Barb was leading the prayer ministry at Christ Community Church in Carmichael, California, where her husband Dave was lead pastor. Christ Community was doing one of the best jobs in the country for reaching people without a church background. (They ranked in the top 150 out of a pool of 30,000 congregations!) It was one of the most effective and inspiring ministries we encountered.

The prayer ministry, and Barb's teaching, lay at the heart of the church. It was one of the most mature and substantial prayer ministries I have every encountered. (If you want to read about it, see chapter 4 of *Unbinding the Gospel: Real Life Evangelism*—a third of the chapter is about the Carmichael prayer ministry. Barb and Dave are called "Beth" and "Don" because of confidentiality agreements in the study.)

Here's the short version: the church was growing deep and wide. Long-term members were growing into more mature versions of the faith. It was healthy. It served its community. New ministries took off and bloomed. Hundreds of new Christians were beginning real faith lives. The church was flexible. Committees could turn on a dime when the Spirit prompted them. And it was fun! Everything they did was grounded in prayer. Barb's teaching and support provided the bedrock for it all. The church was a riveting example of ministry led and empowered by the Spirit.

Those words could be a description of you and of your church in a few years. Churches can come alive again, with prayer and with the help of God. First, we each need to learn how to pray. Our *churches* need to become praying churches. Do you want your life to be more connected with God? Would you like your church to be loving and powerful and really run the race, powered by the Spirit, not by your own exhausted efforts? It's possible. God exists. God loves us dearly. God wants to be in relation with us and to use us. Christ's Spirit will not only comfort us, but will also lead us. The Spirit will bring about shifts and changes we could never anticipate.

We won't become people of prayer accidentally. We won't slip one day and fall into a prayer life. We need a teacher, a coach. We need to *learn* to pray. We keep learning, keep growing, as we continue to pray. Learning prayer takes training, patience, and persistence.

Remember that the apostle Paul compares the Christian life to running a race? Think of Barb as your track coach! Barb is one of the wisest, most humble prayer teachers in the country. I have seen the extraordinary fruits of her teaching in the Carmichael church. You will see the fruits in your own life and in your own church if you and a group of your friends will agree to study *Your Journey to a Prayerful Life*.

Your Journey to a Prayerful Life is insightful, usable, systematic, filled with wisdom. It is infused with Barb's deep knowledge of God, people, and churches. It will change your life and your church if you and a group of friends will use it for real. (Change and new possibilities are comfortable and exciting about 70 percent of the time. Just hang in there with each other for that other amazing 30 percent!)

Christ wants churches and individuals who are learning to know him. Christ needs people who can reach others for him. God loves you more than you can imagine–pray and discover a tiny bit more of the depths of God. Your life can matter more than you know. Your church can enter into a quiet adventure with God, if you'll say yes.

You can't possibly know today what God can do with you in the next year, in the year after that. There is only one question: Are you ready to go?

Martha Grace Reese

Introduction

Writing this study is a result of observing that many in the church, whether new Christians or mature in faith, struggle with how to pray effectively. Over the past several years, I immersed myself in teachings from the Bible, and of other Christian authors, on prayer. Many books have valuable insights, and God used several writers to show me more about Christ and his ways. (See the Bibliography at the end of this book.) Although many authors have written wonderful books and Bible studies about prayer, I couldn't find one that teaches all of the principles that have been most helpful to me and that includes things I deem valuable for others seeking to grow in prayer. I offer this study as an effort to share the many nuggets from different sources God is using to change me. As I was writing, I wondered, "Who needs another study on prayer?" I am not sure I found the answer, but God prompted me to write about the things I'm learning.

God has been changing my life through prayer. He placed a desire in me to move from being a woman who knows how to say a prayer, to living a praying life. God's transforming power continues to operate in my life through prayer. I have discovered that living a praying life is an incredible adventure. I hope that this will be your experience as well!

Considerations for Using This Study

This study is designed with *you* in mind.

This study will encourage you to grow in your intimacy with God by exploring what the Bible teaches about prayer. You will have a key verse to memorize each week. Many of the questions will guide you into scripture. Be sure to read these passages. As you read, ask God to reveal the truth to you. Please remember that studying about prayer should never be a substitute for prayer itself. Every day you will be encouraged to spend some time in prayer. I am learning that many times after I pray and study scripture, God prompts me to some kind of action. A suggested action comes with every daily assignment. Application brings transformation. Learning it leads to living it and finally to loving it. The highest goal for this study is that we come to love Christ more than ever before.

I encourage you to do the daily assignments individually, before you come to the group meeting. You will spend time going over the highlights and questions together in small groups. Typically, the leader will do a wrap-up talk each time you meet, seeking to share other insights from the Word and from how God is shaping and molding him or her.

Begin to pray now that God will use these next weeks to grow you and your group more in love with Jesus as you journey to a prayerful life.

WEEK 1: Foundations of Prayer
DAY 1: *What Is Prayer?*

MEMORY VERSE_____

"Call to me and I will answer you and tell you great and unsearchable things you do not know." JEREMIAH 33:3

To Pray Is to Change

In 1996, I asked God to change me from being a woman who knew how to say a prayer into a woman who lives a praying life. As I came to know more of God and more about prayer, God taught me that prayer is the key to a transformed life. I absolutely cannot be the person God created me to be without having an intimate personal relationship with Christ. Intimacy with God comes with having a dynamic prayer life.

To develop a strong desire and love for prayer and live a praying life, you must learn some basics about prayer. This week, we'll focus on some very basic principles or concepts that will help us as we take this journey to a prayerful life.

Several years ago, I did an Internet search using the word *prayer*. I found more than 125,000 articles on prayer and noticed that Amazon.com listed more than 8,000 books on prayer.

In my own reading I found many definitions of prayer. Here are some of my favorite definitions.

- Prayer is conversation with God.
- Prayer is a relationship, not a religious activity.
- Prayer is our declaration of dependence on God.
- Prayer is the way the life with God is nourished.
- Prayer is a process, not a product.
- Prayer is an invitation to intimacy with God.
- Prayer is not a required spiritual exercise.
- Prayer is the lifeblood of the Christian's relationship with God.
- Prayer is not the words, but the relationship in which I live.
- Prayer is the Christian's vital breath, the Christian's native air.
- The purpose of prayer is not to get what you want, but to become the person God wants you to be.

- The chief object of prayer is to glorify the Lord Jesus.
- To pray is to change.

Think about your experience with prayer. Which definition above most closely fits your belief and practice of prayer?

Which definition provides a new concept about prayer for you?

Why?

Prayer Starts with God

Although we often think of prayer as something we initiate, prayer starts with God. God invites us to pray and places the desire in our heart to have a relationship with Christ nourished by prayer.

O. Hallesby wrote, "Our prayers are always a result of Jesus' knocking at our hearts' doors."[2]

Look up the following scriptures and write about what each one teaches about prayer.

Jeremiah 29:11–14

Jeremiah 33:3

Psalm 141:1–2

Psalm 27:7–8

What does it mean to seek God's face?

What does your current prayer life tell you about your understanding of prayer?

What are your hopes and goals for this study?

PRAY _____

- Praise God for giving you the invitation to pray.
- Praise God for giving you the desire to learn to pray.
- Ask God to strengthen your prayer life.

ACTION _____

Call a friend or family member and ask how that person would define prayer. See if this will encourage a conversation about what prayer means to you.

Week 1: Foundations of Prayer
Day 2: *Why Pray?*

MEMORY VERSE

"Call to me and I will _____ you and _____ _____ great and unsearchable things you do not know." JEREMIAH 33:3

We were created with a great need to be in meaningful relationships. Relationships are often complicated. Parents disappoint us, kids fail us, friends betray us, and spouses don't meet all of our expectations. A relationship with God is different. God wants to know us and bless us. God nourishes and sustains us.

I am thankful that I grew up in a Christian home where I was taught to pray when I was a little girl. Later, I got the message that prayer was a habit that good Christian girls did daily. It was a duty and a discipline, rather than a delight. When prayer was redefined for me so that I discovered the real purpose in prayer, my attitude and approach to prayer changed dramatically. Now I would rather pray than do almost anything else.

Here are some important reasons to pray.

1. God invites and encourages us to pray, and responds to our prayers.

Our key verse this week is Jeremiah 33:3, "Call to me and I will answer you and tell you great and unsearchable things you do not know." Circle the invitation and underline the response.

2. Prayer declares and acknowledges our dependence on God.

Just as Jesus depended on God throughout his earthly ministry, so we depend on God for guidance, insight, protection, and provision. Without God's guidance, which we receive through the Word and prayer, we can't do anything of significance.

Write out John 15:5.

Jesus' brother, James, also taught the importance of depending on God. See James 5:13–16. What is the key idea of these verses?

3. Prayer brings our will in line with the purposes of God.

Read Psalm 32. Notice how the author prays that his life will be in line with God's will. Where applicable, place your name in the verse, (e.g., "I will instruct Barb and teach Barb the way Barb should go..."). Also, see Psalm 37:3–6.

4. Prayer unleashes the storehouse of blessings that God desires to give to those who ask in prayer.

Look up the following verses to find the blessings God has for us. Notice that God's blessings are in line with God's attributes and character. (God is eager to hear from us. God has super-abundant resources. God is generous. God desires the very best for us.)

1 John 5:14–15

Ephesians 1:3

Matthew 6:28–34

Psalm 34:4–8

Psalm 16:11

5. Prayer brings glory and honor to God.

This is probably the most important reason to pray. Prayer is all about God and not about us. Think about how you feel when your child or a friend calls "just because." I always feel so honored when one of our daughters calls just to say "Hi," or to tell me they were thinking of me. When a friend calls, not to ask for a favor, but because she wants to discuss an important decision and requests my advice, I feel very affirmed and valued. God loves to hear from us, just as we love to hear from those who are important to us.

Think of a time you prayed just to tell of your love for God. What were the circumstances and how did you feel about the time spent in prayer?

We have many more reasons to pray, but this should get us going, don't you think?

PRAY _____

- Praise God for inviting you to pray.
- Tell of your desire to depend only on God.
- Confess times when you have tried to live in your own strength.
- Ask God to make your will and purpose for living line up with God's desire for your life.
- Thank God for the blessings generously given to you!
- Spend a few moments today telling God how much you love Christ.

ACTION _____

Take a few moments to reflect on or write about other good reasons to pray

WEEK 1: Foundations of Prayer
DAY 3: *To Whom Do We Pray?*

"Call to _____ and I will answer you and tell you great and unsearchable things you do not know." JEREMIAH 33:3

Have you noticed that people are willing to have you pray for them when they are in a crisis? Have you heard people talking about praying to a "higher power"? Most people are not offended when you offer to pray for them after they tell you about a problem, but many people have no idea to whom we are praying. For the Christian, we can have a clear picture of the One to whom we are praying, for this is revealed to us in God's Word. We don't have to guess about what our "Higher Power" is like and how God will respond to our requests. Today, we will learn about the Holy Trinity as it relates to prayer. Understanding about God the Father, God the Son, and God the Holy Spirit adds great boldness and power to our prayer life.

God the Father

Match the following attributes of God with the appropriate verses:

Compassionate	Genesis 1:1
Creator	Psalm 25:10
Loving	Psalm 103:3
Forgiving	Psalm 103:8
Generous	Psalm 119:137
Holy	Proverbs 3:11–12
Righteous	Matthew 6:11
Disciplinarian	Revelation 4:8

What other attributes of God the Father come to mind?

7

How does knowing these attributes about God, our Father, impact how you pray?

Jesus, God's Son

Look up the following verses and write a characteristic of Christ below each.

Matthew 8:14–17

Matthew 10:1

Matthew 26:36–39

Luke 8:24–25

John 3:16

John 10:14–15

John 14:27

Romans 5:1 & 10

Romans 8:1–2

Hebrews 1:3

After reading about the heart and work of Jesus, how does this understanding affect your prayers?

With Jesus as our high priest, we can come boldly to God with any of our requests. God understands and knows all about that with which we are dealing. Write the key words from Hebrews 4:14–16.

God, the Holy Spirit

What do you know about the Holy Spirit's role in prayer?

Key verses regarding the role of the Holy Spirit in prayer are Romans 8:26–27.
What comfort do you find in these verses?

Jesus said the Holy Spirit gives us life (John 6:63). The Spirit also leads us into truth (John 16:13). The Spirit helps us remember the teachings of Jesus (John 14:26).

The Holy Spirit brings scripture to mind and will guide us and give us the right words to say. Wow! That allows me to be bold in prayer.

Prayer is nothing more than an ongoing and growing love relationship with God the Father, Son, and Holy Spirit. Sometimes we assume that prayer is something to be mastered, like learning to play the piano or becoming an expert in digital photography. That puts us in the "on-top position," according to Richard Foster, where we are competent and in control.[3] When we pray, it is important that we come from the underneath position, bringing ourselves to God, just as we are. The Holy Spirit makes our words acceptable to God, so we can come to God again, and again, and again, in the assurance that a loving God, and Jesus, the powerful and miracle-working high-priest, will hear and answer our feeble prayers. That is good news, isn't it?

PRAY _____

- Praise God for the Father's attributes.
- Thank Jesus for giving you the gift of salvation.
- Ask the Holy Spirit to search your heart so that you will pray in accordance with God's will.
- Pray boldly about a situation for which you have been praying in light of this knowledge of God the Father, the Son, and the Holy Spirit.

ACTION _____

Write out a prayer using some of the verses you looked up today and share it with a friend or relative who struggles with understanding to whom you pray.

WEEK 1: Foundations of Prayer
DAY 4: *Requirements of Prayer*

MEMORY VERSE_____

"Call to me and I will answer you and tell you great and _____*things that you do not know."* JEREMIAH 33:3

In my journey into this life of prayer, I have discovered that although God initiates this relationship with me, I am strengthened and transformed as I apply truths and principles. These three "requirements" continue to be basic as I learn to love and live prayer on a daily basis.

Have an Attitude

When it comes to a healthy prayer life, the right attitude is crucial. This is not the typical attitude we think of when we describe someone as "having an attitude." The right attitude is one of helplessness. This is an attitude of being sorrowful for sin—things I have said and done that were not in line with God's will, and things left undone that would have brought great honor to Christ. Pride and arrogance, the need to be in control, self-centeredness, and other unconfessed sin obstruct prayer. I am learning that it is important to do an "attitude check" when I come to God in prayer.

Does Psalm 66:18–19 confirm the necessity of a right prayer attitude? Write the key words.

Praying in faith, having an attitude of belief in God's availability and power, impacts our prayer life.

Read Mark 11:22–25 and James 1:6 to learn about the relationship between faith, forgiveness, and answered prayer.

Describe your "prayer attitude."

Apply the Name of Jesus

Jesus offers us an amazing privilege by inviting us to pray in his name. It's sort of like being given a blank check with his signature on it, allowing us to draw from his account as we use his resources for his glory. Awesome power rests in the name of Jesus! Often we tack on the phrase "in Jesus' name" at the end of our prayers. This is actually a very good habit. We are authorized to be Christ's representatives as we go to God in Jesus' name. We stand in the place of the Son as we go to the throne of God. Praying in Jesus' name also means that we go to God on the basis of Christ's merit. We go in his authority and purity, having none of this in ourselves. We ask in accord with Christ's will when we pray in Jesus' name. When we pray in Jesus' name, the demons tremble with fear. So whenever we pray, let's be sure to name the name of Jesus. It doesn't matter if it is at the beginning, middle, or end. Awesome power rests in the name of Jesus.

"Until now you have not asked for anything in my name. Ask and you will receive, and your joy will be complete" (John 16:24).

What can you do to learn to be more conscious of Jesus' will as you pray in his name?

Take Action

Obedience is fundamental to an effective prayer life. Did you know that prayerlessness is actually a sin? *Ouch!* At times I cry in shame over my lack of prayer. God's Word clearly teaches we should pray about everything and to pray without ceasing. If I want God to bless me with God's presence and power, I must place myself in a position to tap into those gifts. Prayer can be hard work. I have found myself in a state of exhaustion after extended periods of intercessory prayer. It is not for the faint-hearted.

Some people believe that prayer is only for pious and spiritual people. Some are convinced that God is not interested in hearing from them. Some do not pray, because they are unsure God has power to change people or situations. Some of us don't pray because we have every excuse in the book—too tired, too busy, or too distracted. The list goes on and on. Obedience to a life of prayer is not beyond our reach. God, through the power of the Holy Spirit, gives us the desire, courage, and strength to pray. If you are new to prayer, I say "congratulations" for taking action in learning to love to pray. If you have had a lazy prayer life, in spite of many years as a follower of Jesus, now is the time to "just do it!"

Find encouragement (and maybe a kick in the backside) from these verses. Note how they encourage or challenge you:

1 John 3:21–22

1 John 5:13–15

James 4:2–3

Colossians 1:9–12

Colossians 3:16

John 15:7

What do these verses have in common?

PRAY

- Praise God! God is faithful and just to forgive sin (1 John 1:9).
- Ask God to do an attitude check—confess any sin or disobedience.
- Ask God to increase your faith so that you can pray more powerfully.
- Admit any selfish praying that did not represent the character of Jesus.
- Thank God for amazing promises regarding prayer in the Word.

ACTION

What is God prompting you to do to strengthen and nourish your prayer life? What are you going to do about it? "Just do it!"

WEEK 1: Foundations of Prayer
DAY 5: *The Lord's Prayer*

MEMORY VERSE_____

"Call to me and _____ _____ _____ you and tell you _____ and unsearchable things _____ do not _____." JEREMIAH 33:3

Perhaps the best-known prayer worldwide is the Lord's Prayer, also called the Model Prayer. As Jesus walked and talked with the disciples, they noticed something special about his prayer life. Of all the things the disciples could have asked Jesus to teach them, his closest friends made only one request: that he teach them how to pray. Jesus gave them a comprehensive pattern of prayer. It is a complete prayer.

Do you remember when you learned the Lord's Prayer?

Who taught you to say it? _____

If the person is still alive, write a thank you note to that person this week. It is often the starting point down the path to a prayerful life.

Carefully study and meditate on Matthew 6:9–13.
"Our Father in heaven"
What do you think is the significance of this opening greeting?

Why do we say "our" rather than "my" Father?

14

"Hallowed be your name"

Define the word *hallowed.*

"Your kingdom come, your will be done, on earth as it is in heaven"
This is an important phrase, because it reminds us that God is in charge and we are not. What does it mean to you to ask God for the kingdom of God to come and God's will to be done here and now?

"Give us today our daily bread"
What is daily bread, and why do we need to ask for it one day at a time?

"Forgive us our debts, as we also have forgiven our debtors"
Notice that this is the only part of the prayer that is conditional. Why do you think Jesus links God's forgiveness of us with our forgiveness of others?

"And lead us not into temptation, but deliver us from the evil one"
Rewrite this sentence in your own words.

Many churches close the prayer with the following traditional line:
"For yours is the kingdom, and the power and the glory forever. Amen."
Notice that this summary brings us back to acknowledging who God is and who is in charge. Why is it significant to come back to adoration before we say, "Amen"?

What does "Amen" mean?

This model for prayer can be the basis and backbone of every prayer we verbalize. It is good and right to begin every prayer by speaking God's name and acknowledging one or more of God's attributes. It is also important to seek God's will and guidance when we pray. Because other places in scripture tell us to ask God for what we need, it is consistent that we bring daily needs before God in prayer. Confession of sin relates to the attitude check we spoke of earlier this week, and of our need to be gracious to others, just as God is merciful, forgiving, and kind to us. Whenever we get serious about our relationship with Christ, we will be prime targets for the enemy of God, Satan. Therefore, we need to ask for protection and deliverance from evil influence. As we conclude our prayers, it is important to give God all the credit.

Read Luke 11:1–13 for the context and expansion of Jesus' teaching on prayer. What are the key words/concepts in these verses other than the words of the Lord's Prayer?

"The great beauty of the Lord's Prayer is that it maintains a focus on God. We may be the grammatical object of some sentences there, but we are never the subject; God alone holds that position. Even in confession, we turn our eyes to God and say, You give us bread… You forgive us… You lead us… You deliver us. That kind of prayer provides us with an oft-needed corrective. Perhaps the most subtle temptation, the most persistent evil of all is to stand ourselves in God's rightful place at the center of the landscape of our hearts." [4]

PRAY _____

- Praise God for the pattern of prayer Jesus gave us, his disciples of today.
- Thank God that because of this teaching, we do not have to wonder how we should pray.

ACTION _____

The Lord's Prayer is not meant to be repeated mechanically. A good way to use a model prayer is to take the core idea and expand on it. As you pray it this week, pray with great awe and reverence. Tell God you are glad that you are in God's family with other believers. Pray for someone you know who needs to have the kingdom of God established in his or her heart. Pray for God's will to press in on a situation in your life. Ask God to make it clear to you what you need from God today, and thank God for providing for your basic needs everyday. Confess any known sin to God and make sure your conscience is clear regarding your attitude toward others. Ask the Lord to keep you pure and protected from evil influences and actions. Pray that you will uphold the honor and glory of God's name today. Be willing to share with the group how this "action" affected you.

Week 2: Elements of Prayer
Day 1: *Praise*

MEMORY VERSE_____

"Pray in the Spirit on all occasions with all kinds of prayers and requests. With this in mind, be alert and always keep on praying for all the saints."
EPHESIANS 6:18

People love celebrations. We look for reasons to celebrate. In our culture, we celebrate the agility of professional athletes, the performances of movie stars, and the bravery of heroes. We celebrate birthdays, moms, and apple pie. Sometimes I wonder if we celebrate God's magnificence as much as we do these others. To celebrate means, "to honor and praise publicly." Adoration is the spontaneous desire of the heart to honor, worship, and bless God. Certainly, God deserves honor and praise more than anyone or anything else. Because God is worthy of our praise, beginning our prayers with praise is good.

The Bible is packed with praise. Let's use PRAISE[5] as an acrostic to remember the benefits of praise as we meditate on the associated verses of scripture noted below.

Praise *Preoccupies* Us with God

Praise draws the focus away from our problems and us. It is totally God-centered. It allows us to love God for who God is. It encourages us to set aside our concerns and our prayer lists to focus on enjoying God.

Read these verses and write down common words and phrases they share. Note why each verse praises God.

Psalm 22:23

Psalm 40:3

Psalm 100:4

Psalm103:1

Psalm 146:1–2

Isaiah 6:3

Hebrews 13:15

Revelation 5:11–12

Praise *Recognizes* God's Deeds and Nature

When we verbalize and acknowledge God's greatness, it builds a sense of awe in us. We are telling God we love God. List under each passage what you recognize about God's nature and deeds.

2 Samuel 22:2–4, 32–34, 47, 50

1 Chronicles 16:8–12, 23–29, 31–33

Hebrews 1:10–12

Praise *Agrees* with God's Perspective

When we praise God, our thoughts are brought in line with God's. We view situations the way God sees them, thereby solving some of the mysteries of life. What new reasons to praise God do you find in the verses below?

Proverbs 19:21

Jeremiah 32:17

Daniel 2:20–23

Praise *Invites* the Holy Spirit to Work

Praise creates an atmosphere where the Holy Spirit can do God's work. "God inhabits the praises of His people" (Psalm 22:3).

Describe the role of the Holy Spirit as described in Romans 8:26–28.

Praise *Silences* the Enemy

First Peter 5:8–9 tells us that Satan is like a roaring lion prowling around looking for some victim to devour. "Praise is to Satan what Raid is to bugs."[6] When we praise and adore the Lord, the enemy is quieted and disarmed. When we feel "under attack"—and we will be when we are serious about a love relationship with the Lord—one of our best defenses is to praise and speak the name of Jesus audibly.

What experiences have you had in silencing the enemy? Did you use specific scriptures? How did you praise God?

Praise *Establishes* Faith

Speaking what we know to be true about God builds our faith. The apostle Paul wrote beautiful verses explaining the spiritual blessings we enjoy through faith in Christ.

Read Ephesians 1:3–10 and Philippians 2:6–11. What has Christ done for us?

This is great cause for celebration.

If we could see the heart of God, we would be more apt to regularly praise God. We have a tendency to think that God is so majestic that our adoration makes no difference to God. But God has a tender, sensitive heart and yearns for our gratitude and praise. Remember Jesus' healing of the ten lepers? Only one came back to say thanks. Jesus was moved by the praise of one and saddened by the other nine. Remember the woman who bathed Jesus' feet with her tears and the woman who lavished expensive perfume on Jesus' head? He was touched by their extraordinary acts of adoration. Let's not withhold our praise.

PRAY

- Praise God by telling three things you really appreciate about God.
- Confess times when you have celebrated people and things much less significant than Christ and God's work in your life.
- Ask God to give you even more reasons to adore God—to help you see God's majesty, holiness, and love and to give you a heart to praise God.

ACTION

Choose a praise assignment/experiment and do it a few times over the next week.

1. Praise God with music that focuses on God, who God is, and what God has done. Use corporate worship, Christian radio, favorite CDs, children's music, whatever you like, and sing with all of your heart and voice, making a joyful sound to the Lord!

2. Linger in one or more of these psalms and journal some prayers of praise, allowing the verses to prompt you: Psalm 34; Psalm 95; Psalm 96; Psalm 103.

3. As you go through your daily routine, be aware of the presence and blessing of the Lord, and pause to praise God every hour with a sentence or a song.

WEEK 2: Elements of Prayer
DAY 2: *Confession*

MEMORY VERSE_____

"Pray in the Spirit on all occasions with _____ _____ *of prayers and requests. With this in mind, be alert and always keep on praying for all the saints."* EPHESIANS 6:18

A popular adage says, "Confession is good for the soul." Does that suggest we all have sin to confess?

Read Romans 3:23 and 1 John 1:8. What do these verses tell us about our condition?

While I believe the adage is true, it seems that we settle for living with guilt and shame rather than making time and opportunity for regular self-examination and confession. Have you ever held onto a secret sin or angry resentment until it began to "eat at you"? I have done this more than a few times in my life, but I am learning that holding on to sin, which indeed is no secret to God (and usually not to those close to me either), will not have any benefit to me, physically or spiritually. Sleepless nights, anxiety, lack of peace, stomach pain, feeling far away from God, and mild depression are some of the symptoms I associate with carrying shame and guilt. The psalmist, David, knew the consequences of living with unconfessed sin. Today, we will examine what the Bible teaches about confession and learn about the significant part confession plays in a healthy relationship with God.

Read Psalm 32:1–7. What happened to David when he kept silent about his sin?

What resulted when David confessed his sin?

What does he suggest we do since God is our hiding place and protector and deliverer?

Have you ever felt weak and miserable, or that God's hand of discipline was heavy as a result of your sin? Describe the situation and how you got out of it.

Proverbs 28:13 says that if we try to hide our sins, we will not succeed. How have you learned this lesson?

Find Psalm 51:1–12. Look for key words about confession and forgiveness.

David was haunted by his sin (the background story is found in 2 Samuel 11–12), but confessing the sin drew him back to God. Sadly, many times we have to reach the bottom before we reach the point of confession and turning back to God. At times God can use our sin, our shame, our guilt, and our despair to bring us closer to God. True confession leads to forgiveness, freedom from guilt and shame, and the restoration of joy and gladness.

See Psalm 30:11–12 and Romans 4:7–8. What words and actions describe the forgiven person?

Look at what occurs when a believer confesses and is truly sorry for sin.

1 John 1:9

Psalm 103:11–13

How are you doing with regular times of examination, confession, and repentance? I have discovered a few exercises that have helped me in being honest before God. I tend to use my morning shower to ask God to cleanse me from sin, wrong attitudes, motives, thoughts, and actions that are displeasing to God. As I wash the perspiration and soil off my body, I visualize God cleansing me from the stain of sin. It goes down the drain. I am free and pure!

At other times as I walk, I will ask God to reveal sin in my life, that of which I may not be aware. As I am quiet and alone with God, God often brings something to my mind. With God doing the search with me, I am kept from rationalization ("Oh, it wasn't really that bad, was it?") or self-loathing ("What a miserable wretch I am!"). God's mercy and grace is balanced with God's expectations for me, and I have no fear of asking God to reveal my weaknesses and faults.

Keeping a journal has also been helpful in keeping me honest with God. When words are in black and white, my sin seems very real. Sometimes after confessing and being in sorrow over my sin, I tear the page out of the journal and toss it into the trash, symbolizing that this is a sin God has forgiven, and one that I have no intention of repeating.

Knowing that sin is an issue for us, and understanding the value of confession, match the verses with the application/action below. Write the appropriate letter beside the verse. These verses offer preventative measures to keep us from sinning.

____2 Chronicles 7:14   a. Don't love the world

____Romans 6:12–14   b. Humble ourselves and pray

____Hebrews 12:1–2   c. Keep our eyes fixed on Jesus

____James 4:7   d. Offer ourselves to God

____1 John 2:15–17   e. Submit to God and resist the devil

True confession will lead you into a deeper love relationship with God. Don't avoid it. Don't miss the freedom and joy that God wants to give you.

PRAY

- Praise God for God's mercy, which means God does not treat us as we deserve.
- Thank the Lord for symptoms of unconfessed sin that drive us into God's arms.
- Ask for a clean heart and a renewed spirit.

ACTION

Try one of the three confession exercises mentioned this week.

1. Cleansing shower
2. Examination walk
3. Journaling

WEEK 2: Elements of Prayer
DAY 3: *Petition*

MEMORY VERSE_____

"Pray in the spirit on _____ occasions with _____ kinds of prayers and requests. With this in mind, be alert and always keep on praying for all the saints." EPHESIANS 6:18

In the context of this study, petition is asking God for our personal needs. I cannot emphasize enough how much God wants to bless your life through answered prayer. It is amazing to consider that the God of the whole universe chooses to answer our individual prayers! God answers them because God loves us and delights in our asking. Some people think that asking for things for one's self is selfish and unspiritual, but that thinking does not line up with scripture. In fact, both the Hebrew and Greek words for prayer mean "to request." We learn from the Bible that asking, this dependency on God, is primary throughout our lives. Our asking warms the heart of God.

Saint Teresa of Avila said, "You pay God a compliment by asking great things of him."[7]

Look up the following verses to find encouragement to ask God to meet your needs.

Matthew 7:7–8, "_____ and it will be given to you; _____ and you will find; _____ and it will be opened to you."

James 4:2d, "You do not have, because you do not _____."

Philippians 4:19, "God will meet _____ your needs according to his glorious riches in Christ Jesus."

Luke 11:3, "_____ us each day our daily _____."

Psalm 5:3, "Morning by morning I lay my _____ before you and wait in expectation."

Faith is built by watching and seeing how God answers prayer for our personal needs. Whether the need is large or small, it matters to God. The Lord delights in hearing from us.

A few common problems surrounding prayers of petition occasionally keep us from praying. Have you ever wondered why we should ask God for things God already knows? The easiest answer to that question is that God likes to be asked. The mere asking deepens the relationship. Second, we wonder whether we should bother God with our problems. After all, God has a big world to look after. The rule of thumb here is, if something is causing us any amount of distress, it is worth talking to God about it. Finally, people fear that they will ask God for something contrary to God's will. Odds are that we will. The Bible teaches us principles that will help us in knowing how to ask when we come to God with our personal needs.

Read the following verses and write the keys to praying effectively for personal needs.

2 Chronicles 16:9

Psalm 37:4

Proverbs 3:5–6

Matthew 6:33

John 15:7

1 John 5:14–15

First John 3:21–22 tells us that if we expect God to do what we ask, we should be prepared to do for God what is asked of us. This is the obedience factor. Take a moment to think about what it means for you to "delight yourself in the Lord."

What does it look like for you to "seek first the kingdom of God"? How are you doing in this area?

How is it going for you regarding trusting God with all your heart? Do you turn to God first when you have a problem, or do you call a friend for advice first?

Faith is a key element in praying effectively for ourselves. James says when we ask God we must really expect God to answer. If we don't believe that God has power or ability to impact the situation that concerns us, we are less likely to talk with God about it, and God is less likely to act. Pray with confidence.

It is helpful to be reminded of the character of God as we come to the Lord with our requests. See Matthew 7:9–11. What kind of gifts does God like to give?

Review the role of Christ in prayer—Jesus understands and cares (Hebrews 4:15–16). The kind of gifts that Jesus gives includes the spiritual blessings of wisdom, joy, peace, power, Christlike character, etc. These are always in line with God's will. When we ask for good things like these, we will begin to see God working those into our lives. When we are unsure about whether our petitions are in line with God's will, we can ask God to reveal it through the Bible, through the wise counsel of a mature Christian, and by placing confidence in the guidance and direction of the Holy Spirit.

Are you praying for yourself with confidence? Are you asking God for good gifts such as spiritual blessings, as well as for physical provision?

Before you pray for your needs today, consider this picture of how God views you.

"The LORD your God is with you,
  he is mighty to save.
He will take great delight in you,
  he will quiet you with his love,
  he will rejoice over you with singing" (Zephaniah 3:17).

PRAY _____

- Thank God for the promise to provide for all of your needs.
- Confess times when you have failed to ask for the riches God has promised you.
- Ask God for spiritual blessings of faith, joy, peace, wisdom, and love today.

ACTION _____

Begin to keep a prayer diary to record what you request of God. Be aware of the kinds of things you request, and begin recording the answers.

At the top of the first page, write this prayer from Julian of Norwich (fourteenth century):

"God, of your goodness, give me yourself; for you are sufficient for me. I cannot properly ask anything less, to be worthy of you. If I were to ask less, I should always be in want. In you alone do I have all. Amen."[8]

WEEK 2: Elements of Prayer
DAY 4: *Intercession*

MEMORY VERSE_____

"Pray in the Spirit on all occasions with all kinds of prayers and requests. With this in mind, be alert and always _____ _____ _____ _____ _____ the saints." EPHESIANS 6:18

Intercession means praying for others. Praying for others is a love ministry. It is both a great privilege and a serious responsibility. In the ongoing mission of God's kingdom, few things are as important as intercessory prayer. Praying for others has brought me great joy throughout my lifetime. I have felt connected to people I dearly love through prayer, even though many miles separate us. I have seen miracles happen in people and in churches as a result of intercessory prayer. I have witnessed instantaneous answers to prayers offered on behalf of others, and I have prayed for years, waiting with fellow believers for God to bring Christ's presence and power to bear on specific situations. I am sure of this: God hears and answers prayers of intercession!

What person or situation do you pray for regularly?

An intercessor is a go-between or mediator. Intercessors go to God on behalf of others. Jesus tells a story about a "friend-in-the-middle." Read Luke 11:5–8. Notice the friend-in-the-middle pleads on behalf of the one who has nothing. God is the friend with the bread and responds to the boldness of the friend-in-the-middle.

Many people desperately need our intercessory prayers. Families are dysfunctional. Neighbors are lonely and isolated. Thousands are sick, hungry, or unemployed. Millions live without the hope of Christ. All of these people need much more than we will ever be able to give them, but God can meet every need. God has chosen us to be "friends-in-the-middle" to our hurting world.

Sometimes I try to imagine God determining what will happen in the life of my family, friends, and church on the basis of my prayers on their behalf. This is a rather daunting thought, and yet it reminds me of the importance of my role as an intercessor. At times I imagine God's activity in response to my prayers. My simple prayers can release blessing or bring change anywhere in the world without me even leaving my home. This is not because of me, but because God's power is so awesome. God's power is at work through my prayer, because Jesus has an ongoing ministry of intercession at the right hand of God. He is the *real* "friend-in-the-middle" praying at the right hand of God, interpreting my feeble prayers, and making them acceptable to a holy God. The intercessory work of Christ also sustains my desire to pray and gives me hope.

Look at 1 Timothy 2:1–4 to discover for whom we are to pray.

What are we to pray for on their behalf?

PRAY

At times, I become overwhelmed with the needs around me, so I frequently use an acrostic, using the word *BLESS*.[9] This is not original with me, but it is meant to be shared. I am praying that it will be useful for you. The "Pray" and "Action" portions of today's assignment are wrapped up in this *BLESS* format. Please take time to use it to pray for a special friend or family member this week.

B is for Body. Pray for health, protection, strength, and fitness. Use Matthew 6:25–34 as a guide, and pray that God, who sends every good and perfect gift, will meet physical needs. *Pray:* Lord, may _____ seek your kingdom first and discover that food, clothing, health, and safety are given to *her/him* as well. May _____ recognize you as the giver of all of these physical gifts and praise you.

L is for Labor. Pray for meaningful work, sufficient income, and financial security. Use Colossians 3:23–24 as a model in praying about labor. *Pray:* Lord, today I pray that _____ will be diligent in their work with a sense of serving you in all they do, aware of the inheritance prepared for them through all eternity. Give them some assignments today that will cause them to rely on your power and not on their own abilities. Cause them to be joyful and glad that you are providing financially for their families. (If you are praying for people who are unemployed, pray that the Lord will provide meaningful work that will utilize their God-given gifts and bring great honor to God.)

E is for Emotional. Pray for the inner life—for joy, peace, stability, self-control, etc. 1 Peter 5:7 tells us to cast all of our anxieties on Christ because he cares for us. Galatians 5:22–23 lists the fruit of the Spirit. Look up these verses, and insert the name of a person for whom you want to "stand in the middle" today. Pray that the person will be aware of the Lord's desire to fill him or her, so that this person's life exhibits the fruit.

S is for Social. Pray for relationships: marriage, family, friends, co-workers, and neighbors. Proverbs 17:17 states: "A _____ loves at all times." Thank God for a network of supportive friends and co-workers. In Matthew 19:19, Jesus said, "Love your _____ as [you love] _____." Pray for a heart to love your neighbors, even if they have offended you or forgot to return the ladder you loaned them, or if their cat prowls around your pool. In praying about marriages, Hebrews 13:4 teaches us that all should honor marriage. Also read what the apostle Paul taught about marriage in Ephesians 5:33. Pray for a marriage that is struggling. *Pray:* Lord, instill great love in _____'s heart for his wife and fill _____'s mind with great respect for her husband. Pray for married people to continue to honor their vows.

S is for Spiritual. Pray for salvation for unbelievers and spiritual growth for Christians. In praying for unsaved friends or neighbors, ask that their eyes may be opened and their heart may be softened to spiritual things. (We will spend a day on praying for the lost later in this study.) As you pray for Christians, use this prayer of Paul in Colossians 1:9–12, substituting a specific name for the word "you."

ACTION

Use the *BLESS* acrostic to pray for particular people God has placed in your heart. You may use one person throughout the acrostic or a different person with each letter.

Week 2: Elements of Prayer
Day 5: *Thanksgiving*

MEMORY VERSE_____

"_____ in the Spirit on all occasions with all _____ of prayers and requests. With this in mind, be alert and always keep on praying for all the saints." EPHESIANS 6:18

Thanksgiving is the twin sister to praise. It may seem hard to separate the two. They are a lot alike, but they are not identical. In adoration and praise, we focus on who God is. In thanksgiving, we focus on what God has done.

Have you noticed that gratitude is a learned behavior? I remember my parents prompting my brother, sister, and me to say "thank you" whenever we were served a meal at someone's home or when a gift was given at Christmas. We needed reminders, because saying thanks did not come naturally. Even adults need to learn to be thankful.

As we consider this final basic and important element of prayer, it will be helpful to immerse ourselves in the Psalms where the writers concentrate on the mighty works of God.

What are the works of God for which the psalmist is thankful?

Psalm 95:1–7

Psalm 98:1–9

Psalm 100:4–5

Psalm 105:1–3

Psalm 107:1

What are the works of God for which you are thankful?

It is enjoyable to be around people who have grateful hearts. They tend to notice little kindnesses and gestures of good will on the part of others and on the part of God. They also maintain an attitude of gratitude in spite of hardship and adversity. They are able to thank God for "Plan B" even when they may have preferred "Plan A." I love being with people who have moved from "thanks-giving" to "thanks-living." This continues to be a growing edge for me.

Let's find encouragement from these New Testament verses. Discover what it takes to make the transition from "thanks-giving" to "thanks-living."

Philippians 1:3: "I _____ my God every time I remember you."

Philippians 4:6: " Do not be anxious about anything, but in everything, by prayer and petition, with _____, present your requests to God"

Colossians 4:2: "Devote yourselves to prayer, being watchful and _____."

1 Thessalonians 5:18: "Give _____ in all circumstances, for this is God's will for you in Christ Jesus."

Hebrews 12:28: "Since we are receiving a kingdom that cannot be shaken, let us be _____, and so worship God acceptably with reverence and awe."

Luke 22:17a, 19a: "After taking the cup, [Jesus] gave _____ And he took bread, gave _____ and broke it."

1 Corinthians 15:57: "But _____ be to God! He gives us the victory through our Lord Jesus Christ."

What strikes you about these verses?

Is thanksgiving an option for the Christian? _____

On a scale of 1–10, how would you rate your attitude of gratitude?

Jesus lived a life of thanks to God. As we learn to love to live a life of prayer, thanksgiving needs to be woven into the very fabric of our lives. Our thanks to God will bring great honor to God and will keep our hearts light and free.

Lloyd Ogilvie wrote, "Prayers of gratitude, renewed everyday and motivated by the cross, will keep us going. We can be generous in giving our time, money and energy when fueled by the realization of how much we have been loved." [10]

PRAY _____

- Confess an attitude of discontent or ungratefulness and confess times when you have forgotten to say thanks to the Lord for answered prayer.
- Thank God for all that God has done for you—including forgiveness of sin and salvation.
- Thank God for all that God has given you, including physical, relational, and spiritual blessings.
- Thank God for the hardships and suffering you have experienced that have drawn you closer to God's heart.

ACTION _____

Over the next several days, say thank you to everyone who assists you in any way, big or small. Take time to write a note of thanks or send an e-mail to thank someone who has done something to enrich your life. Make a list of everything in which you are thankful to God and tell someone about the "mighty acts of God" in your life.

WEEK 3: Tools for Effective Prayer
DAY 1: *Prayer Closet*

MEMORY VERSE_____

"Let us then approach the throne of grace with confidence, so that we may receive mercy and find grace to help us in our time of need."
HEBREWS 4:16

If you've been around Christians awhile, you may have heard about "daily quiet time" or having a "prayer closet." This concept comes from the teaching of Jesus in Matthew 6:6. I like how it is presented in *The Message*. Jesus says, "Here's what I want you to do: Find a quiet, secluded place so you won't be tempted to role-play before God. Just be there as simply and honestly as you can manage. The focus will shift from you to God, and you will begin to sense his grace." According to this verse, the "prayer closet" experience allows for being relaxed, with "comfortable in my own skin" kind of conversation. Jesus really gives permission for us to be ourselves with our Savior.

Someone once said, "The secret to a powerful prayer life is having a secret place." The purpose of time spent with God is to build a deeper love relationship with God, so let the love of God and the joy of the Lord fill your place of prayer. It is really helpful to set aside a place in your home for prayer, Bible reading, and reflection. I have a special prayer chair in a room free of other distractions. I used to have it in our home office, but as I began to do more computer work, the computer became a distraction, so I moved it to another place. Some people have a room, others a special chair, and others have a spot in their backyard. Some consider their cars to be places of prayer, especially if they have long commutes. One woman has decorated an imaginary room in her mind. As she travels, she goes to that place of prayer, no matter where she is geographically.

Notice where Jesus went to pray:

Mark 1:35

Luke 5:16

Luke 6:12

Do you have a "prayer closet"? If so, where is it?

Who and what you pray for in your prayer closet usually includes the elements of prayer we learned about last week. It is important to pray in a way so that God will be pleased and honored by the time you spend with the Lord. Just as there are a variety of personalities, so there are a variety of styles for prayer closets. If you are a morning person, you probably spend time alone with God in the morning. If you are a night owl, perhaps your best time with God is spent in the quietness before you go to bed at night.

Read Psalm 5:3 to discover when David prayed.

See Daniel 6:10 to learn when Daniel prayed.

When is the best time of day for you?

If you are a visual person, perhaps you are assisted by images, such as a lit candle to represent the presence of Christ, pictures of those you are praying for, or maps of countries for which you pray. If you are a passionate worshiper, perhaps you benefit from using praise music in your prayer time to lead you to more effective praise. If you are a writer, you probably use a prayer journal and record your prayers and God's responses to them. Perhaps you are an organizer, so you like to use prayer lists or prayer calendars to keep you on track in praying for people or situations. If you tend to be emotional, you may "cry buckets" when you are alone in prayer, so keep the tissues nearby!

What about prayer posture? Do you pray on your knees, seated in a comfortable chair, or lying on the floor? Are your hands folded or open on your lap, or arms raised to heaven? Are your eyes opened or closed? No one prayer posture is more correct than others. The key is to be in a position where you can comfortably meet with God.

How much time should Christians spend everyday in their prayer closets? I believe some Christian teachers have dangerously dictated an amount of time needed for obedient disciples of Jesus. Some say you must have at least thirty minutes, while others claim it is not very worthwhile if you don't devote one hour each day. I don't believe it is helpful to be legalistic in this matter. I think primarily two things determine the amount of time needed in our prayer closets. First, spend enough time to build a strong love relationship with Christ. The psalmist says, "You will fill me with joy in your presence, / with eternal pleasure at your right hand" (Psalm 16:11). If my time with Christ is not filling me up so that I experience the love and joy of the Lord, then that is an indicator that I need more time with God. The second factor to consider is what is going on in my life at this time. While I believe it is essential to spend quality alone time with Christ everyday, I know that God is fully aware of what we are experiencing in our lives. When you have young children who are demanding or when you are ill, it may not be possible to devote thirty to sixty minutes daily in spending time with God. Just be sure that you are continuing to grow more and more in love with Jesus. As you do this, you will desire more and more time with God.

Look up these verses to find the benefits of spending time with Christ.
Psalm 21:6

Psalm 16:8–11

PRAY

- Praise God for the joy of being in God's presence every day.
- If spending time with God daily has not been a priority, confess that now.
- Ask God to give you the desire and the discipline to establish a prayer closet.

ACTION

If you don't already have a prayer closet, take time to arrange a place in your home this week and determine what time of day, how much time you'd like to spend there, and what tools you'll use for effective prayer (e.g., candle, journal, etc.)

WEEK 3: Tools for Effective Prayer
DAY 2: *Praying Scripture*

MEMORY VERSE_____

"Let us then approach the _____ _____ _____ *with confidence,
so that we may receive mercy and find grace to help us in our time of need."*
HEBREWS 4:16

The Bible is God's love letter to us. It reveals God's plans and purposes. The scripture is at the very heart of knowing God intimately. It delights God when we read, sing, and pray the Word. For me personally, learning to pray scripture has been the single most important tool in strengthening, enhancing, and empowering my life of prayer.

"Praying Scripture" involves using scripture passages to stimulate prayer. Here are some benefits of praying the Word.

- Praying scripture keeps our prayer life fresh. It gets us out of the rut of using all the words we routinely or mechanically pray.
- Praying scripture helps us become aware of God's purposes and desires. It allows us to shift our focus from ourselves to God. It prompts us to action.
- Praying scripture allows the attributes of God to come alive. It reminds us of God's power, faithfulness, provision, love, and goodness.
- Praying scripture helps the Bible become vital. It becomes an expression of our heart and becomes part of our own story as we identify with joys, struggles, and needs of biblical characters.
- Praying scripture enhances personal worship. Praise, adoration, and confession come alive through the Bible.
- Praying scripture helps us meditate and memorize the Word. Its truth takes root in our souls.
- Praying scripture allows us to know and claim the promises in the Word.

We tend to think of prayer as a monologue, but when we pray with an open Bible, we establish a dialogue. Prayer is meant to be a dialogue between the believer and God–two-way communication. Today, we'll use several passages of scripture to prompt our prayers, and we will use scripture in different ways.

1. Pray the Psalms

The best-loved prayer book is the book of Psalms. The Psalms evoke great passion and feeling. Read these three psalm passages and write prayers prompted by the verses you read and my suggestions.

Psalm 95:1–7: I praise you Lord! I sing for joy because you saved me. You are a great God.

Psalm 32:1–7: You bless me Lord by forgiving my sin. I have kept silent about _____. Today I want to confess that to you. I am tired of covering up things I have done wrong. These include:

Psalm 13:1–2, 5–6: Lord, I feel like you have forgotten me. How long do I have to wrestle with _____? Please answer me Lord.

I will trust in your love. Thanks for being _____.

2. Pray the Gospels

You can use the Beatitudes in Matthew 5 or parables found throughout the New Testament. Pray the narrative by personalizing the passage. Put yourself in the story. Read Mark 4:35–41, and pray about an area of your life that is causing you fear. Pray that you will become aware of Jesus' presence and ask him to calm the storm.

Read Matthew 5:9. "Blessed are the peacemakers, / for they will be called [children] of God." Personalize these words of Jesus by praying, "Lord, I pray that I will trust you to work through me to resolve the conflict between _____ and _____. Thank you for showing me the kind of character people in your kingdom possess."

3. Pray the Prayers of the Bible

The Bible contains dozens of prayers. Some are very short: one sentence. Others comprise entire chapters. It is helpful to understand who is writing the prayer and the context. We don't want to bend scripture to suit our own needs. Observe the passage first, then interpret it, and finally apply it to your situation.

Pray Solomon's prayer for wisdom from 1 Kings 3:9. Ask the Lord for wisdom or discernment in a situation you are facing.

Pray Paul's prayer found in Ephesians 1:16–23. Insert a name or a group into the paragraph as you think about other Christians who have influenced your faith journey.

Use Paul's prayer as a way to thank God for them and to pray for their needs.

4. Pray the Promises to Gain Victory over Recurrent Sin

Pray 2 Corinthians 10:3–5 as a powerful tool to gain victory over thoughts that may lead us to sin.

5. Personalize Scripture to Apply to Your Life Situation

Read the following, and write the topic that these verses can be used to pray about.

Joshua 1:6–9

Psalm 23

Psalm 34:7

Matthew 11:28–31

Romans 15:4–6

1 Corinthians 13

Philippians 4:6–7

Philippians 4:8–9

PRAY _____

- Praise God for the power of the Word.
- Ask for the desire to learn to pray scripture.

ACTION _____

Begin to implement using scripture in your prayer closet at least once each week. Notice how it changes your life of prayer!

WEEK 3: Tools for Effective Prayer
DAY 3: *Listening Prayer*

MEMORY VERSE_____

"Let us then _____ the throne of grace with confidence, so that we may receive mercy and find grace to help us in our time of need." HEBREWS 4:16

Prayer is a dialogue between the believer and God–two-way communication. In listening prayer, we listen more than we speak. Our praying isn't really complete until we adequately listen to God. (A more advanced form of listening prayer is called contemplative prayer.) Listening prayer can be part of every believer's daily experience. Jesus listened to God and taught the importance of such listening. See John 10:14–16, 27.

When we pray, to listen is probably more important than to speak. God really has more to say than we do. Sometimes we are concerned about whether God hears our prayers, but I believe more often God says, "Can you hear me now?" Before we rush into God's presence with our prayer plan, let's be attentive to what God is trying to say to us. This requires some quiet–and God awareness. The better we know the shepherd, the more sure we will be of God's voice. Who does the most talking in your prayer life? Read Luke 10:38–41.

What did Mary do when Jesus visited her home?

What did Martha do?

What did Jesus say was the better way?

Are you more like Martha or Mary?

When we listen to God, we receive guidance from the Holy Spirit. If I am to have a relationship with God that is real and personal, I must be open to the possibility that sometimes God speaks directly to me. I have never heard an "audible voice," but I frequently receive promptings or leadings from the Holy Spirit. In past times of silence, God has "spoken" to me about:

"Forgive the wedding coordinator who made big mistakes at Kara's wedding."

"I have a plan and purpose for you—so make a home for these two daughters of a drug-addicted mother."

"Be a prayer coordinator."

"Befriend your widowed neighbor."

If I had not listened to God's voice, I would have missed out on conviction, assurance of love, and assignments that were life changing.

When has God spoken to you?

Did God give words of comfort/conviction/challenge/love/support? Circle those that apply.

Listening to God is often effective when we are praying scripture. Read these passages to learn how God uses the Bible to speak to us:

Romans 10:17

2 Timothy 3:16–17

2 Peter 1:21

God also speaks to us in other ways. See these verses and write how God speaks.

1 Kings 19:12–13

Psalm 8

Isaiah 30:21

Romans 2:14–15

2 Timothy 1:5–6

In our culture, we equate quiet, solitude, "time out," and solitary confinement with punishment. We go to great lengths to avoid loneliness or being alone. Biblically, however, solitude has great value. Think of it as solitary *refine*ment. Richard Foster wrote, "The post-modern person is addicted to haste, hurry, hustle. And the addiction shrivels our soul... [I]t becomes nearly impossible for us to obey the divine whisper, 'Be still and know that I am God' (Psalm 46:10). Some things will not yield to our perpetual hankering for the instant, immediate, or the sudden. Surely the growth of our soul before God is one of those things."[11]

Take a break from noise and read Psalm 46.

PRAY _____

- Praise the Shepherd who speaks so that we may hear and follow God's voice.

- Thank God for speaking to us through the Word, the Holy Spirit, and other believers.
- Confess personal failure or lack of desire in listening to God.
- Spend time in silent prayer.

ACTION

Since listening prayer is unnatural for most of us, I offer the following suggestions for developing this tool.

- *Practice silence.* Turn off the radio, MP3 player, and TV. Allow enough time to be quiet before God. We usually don't listen well when our surroundings are noisy and we are in a hurry. Take three slow, deep breaths before you start to pray. Relax your body and get comfortable. Take a walk alone in a quiet place and ask God to reveal more of God's self to you, or ask who needs prayer. Then wait to see what visual images God brings to your mind.
- *Watch for God's promptings throughout the day.* If God wakes you in the middle of the night for no apparent reason, ask for whom you need to pray. As a face comes to your mind, pray for that person. If you have an unexpected change in schedule during the day with a few unanticipated extra minutes, ask God if this time was created for a specific purpose. If suddenly you are prompted to call a friend to offer encouragement, do it!
- *Begin with posing a question or a problem to God.* Perhaps after you read a portion of scripture, you are faced with uncertainty or questions. Ask God about it, and then begin to look for God's answers all day long. If we don't ask the question, we miss the answer God is waiting to give!

Whenever we hear something, we should validate it with the Bible before we act on it. A "word from the Lord" will always resonate with other believers who are in prayer and in the Word, and it must be relevant to the situation or issue at hand.

WEEK 3: Tools for Effective Prayer
DAY 4: *Continual Prayer*

"Let us then approach the throne of grace with _____, so that we may receive mercy and find _____ to _____ us in our time of need."
HEBREWS 4:16

When I asked Jesus to transform my life, he began to teach me what it means to pray without ceasing, or as Paul wrote, "Pray continually" (1 Thessalonians 5:17). Our memory verse last week taught us to "pray...on _____ occasions" (Ephesians 6:18). Paul also wrote "Devote yourselves to prayer" (Colossians 4:2).

How do you define unceasing or continual prayer?

Praying continually does not mean that we are to do nothing but pray. It means that we live with an awareness of the presence of God every hour of every day. It means walking and talking with God. Think of having God as your traveling companion as you journey through life. The best part of a trip is often conversation with those traveling with us regarding sights we see, experiences we share, and decisions we make. Life with God is similar—there is a lot to talk about together as we experience life, and, although we can't see or touch God, God is our companion and guide. God is experiencing life with us.

Continual prayer is as natural as breathing in air. Prayer comes naturally to our spirit when our spirit cooperates with the Spirit of God. Remember, prayer is not only the words we say, but the relationship we live in. Write out Acts 17:28.

Praying continually means weaving prayer with activity–making it a habit to talk to God about everyday experiences, enjoying God's presence throughout the day. Here is a sample day devoted to unceasing prayer. Notice the "*prayer triggers.*" They are routine habits that prompt prayer.

Waking up–"Thank you, Lord, for restful sleep and a new day!"

Morning shower–"Lord, wash me clean as this shower cleanses my body."

"Prayer closet" time–time to read the Bible, pray, and journal.

Walk/Exercise–time to listen to God and pray for needs around me.

Breakfast–prayer of thanks for food.

Brushing teeth–"Thanks for clean, safe drinking water" and prayer for people who don't have this convenience.

Getting kids ready for school–pray with them about their day, for their teacher, friends.

Commute to work–prayer for safety in traffic; blessing on co-workers; productive, meaningful work to do.

Waiting at traffic lights–use stops to remind me that God loves me and I love God!

Lunch–thanks for food and praying for our country and its leaders

Hear a siren–"Lord, give paramedics, firemen, and those they are serving all they need."

Placed on "hold" on the phone–pray for our church's office staff.

Hear a coworker tell about marriage problem–pray silently for God to work in her marriage to bring reconciliation.

Getting in the car–thanks for sturdy, safe transportation.

Listening to praise music in the car–praising God in song all the way home.

Preparing dinner–thanks for provision of money and food.

Watching TV news–startling report that upsets–bring it to God in prayer, that he will reveal his purposes and plans in this situation.

The children are fighting–pray for wisdom as you teach about kindness and love.

Phone call from a friend or family member–before saying good-bye, offer a prayer.

Attending a class at church–pray for the teacher and all who attend; ask for the teaching of the Holy Spirit, for new and meaningful insights

Vacuumed the family room and folded a load of laundry–pray for your spouse.

Bedtime–review the day with God. Anything to confess, anything to surrender? What am I grateful for?

What about combining daily activity with prayer seems difficult to you?

What benefits might there be for you in living like this?

To develop this process of continual prayer, take one step at a time. Continual prayer is about developing an awareness of God; *it is not about works,* or feeling pressure to remember to pray constantly. We focus on God and the task until they are blended together. We pray more *process-oriented prayer* and fewer *results-oriented prayer.* Continual prayer is great time management. We avoid compartmentalizing our lives–time for God, time for play, time for work, etc. Every minute has been given to God. We develop an attitude of gratitude when we live in unbroken fellowship with Christ. Our conversations and actions become "holy ground." We have partnered with God throughout the day!

I love this quote from Dallas Willard: "The indirect result of prayer on the conduct of our lives is obvious and striking. The effect of conversing with God can't fail to have a pervasive and spiritually strengthening effect on all aspects of our personality. The more we pray, as we see results, our confidence in God's power spills over into the other areas of our life."[12]

PRAY _____

- Praise God that the Lord enjoys your companionship all through the day.
- Confess the bad habit of leaving God out of your thoughts and actions, feelings and experiences.
- Ask God to help you pray continually.
- Pray that a loved one will also desire to walk and talk with God.

ACTION _____

Think of prayer triggers that might prompt you to pray.

Write a sample day of continual prayer to fit your lifestyle.

Week 3: Tools for Effective Prayer
Day 5: *Team Prayer*

"Let _____ then approach the throne of grace with confidence, so that _____ may receive mercy and find grace to help _____ in _____ time of need." HEBREWS 4:16

Prayer is always personal; but sometimes it is private, and sometimes it is corporate. Group prayer is important when we consider living a praying life. Group prayer was the driving force of the Acts church. Jesus had prayer partners throughout his ministry. At times he engaged in small group prayer. Jesus promises to be present in great power whenever people come together in his name. Praying with others—whether partnering with one other person, a small group, or with a large group of believers—brings huge benefits.

Read the following passages and indicate the value of team prayer.

Ecclesiastes 4:9–12

Mark 14:32–38

Luke 1:39–45

Acts 1:12–14

Acts 2:42–47

What happens when we pray with others?

It links people together. Deep relationships are formed by praying with and for each other. I have had the privilege of having several different prayer partners through the years. Some of my best friends are women I have prayed with on a regular basis. When seeking a prayer partner, look for a same-sex person who will keep confidences, someone who loves you enough to listen to your heart confessions and bring your needs to God in confidence. Prayer partnerships are ruined by gossip or broken trust. Burdens are divided, and joys are multiplied when others pray for us and with us.

Prayer partners can meet weekly for prayer, e-mail prayers, or pray over the phone. (If you have been uncomfortable praying audibly with others, having a prayer partner you are comfortable with will help in this area.) You will want at least one ongoing prayer partner, and then perhaps a prayer group to support you in certain seasons of responsibility or stress. Don't go through life changes or take on new areas of ministry without a team praying for you daily for protection, strength, faith, blessing, etc.

Do you have a prayer partner?
How has he or she blessed your life?

Consistency in prayer develops. When you have a prayer group that meets weekly or monthly, accountability and regularity is built in. If you struggle with the discipline of prayer, being part of a group is helpful. If you feel like giving up in praying for a difficult situation, the group will help you to persist.

Have you participated in a prayer group?
How has it benefited you?

The huge task of intercession becomes more manageable. If you have a heart for people, you may be prone to feeling overwhelmed by all the needs that require prayer. When you pray with others, you discover that you don't have to pray about every situation, because God prompts people to pray for different things. Certain women with whom I pray always pray for marriages and families. Others pray for government. Someone else prays for the strong witness of the church, while another has a heart for unsaved friends. When we come together to pray, we find a sense of great accomplishment in bringing all these needs to God's throne.

What have you learned by listening to the prayers of others?

Our faith is strengthened. It is uplifting to praise God with others. When we pray with others in unity and see how God answers prayer, we are reminded of God's great power, care, compassion, and love. When people share how God has been working in their lives or how God answered prayers, our faith is bolstered.

Write of a time when your faith grew as a result of answered prayer—when someone prayed for you or with you.

It leads to renewal and revival. Historically, revivals took place following times of corporate prayer. A church in revival loves to be in the presence of God. Corporate prayer meetings in our country have declined because of rugged individualism, busyness, and boring request-based prayer. To have a meaningful, powerful group prayer experience, it is vital to have spirit-led, worship-fed prayer. This means being sensitive to the presence of the Holy Spirit through scripture, song, and prayer. We seek God's face before we seek God's hand. Instead of coming to God with our requests, the question asked is, "Jesus, what are your requests?" We trust that as we pray together, our church will be renewed.

What experiences have you had with corporate prayer?

Attend a corporate prayer gathering the next time one is scheduled at your church.

"My house will be called
   a house of prayer for all nations." (Isaiah 56:7)

"God rules the world and his church through the prayers of his
   people."[13]

PRAY _____

- Praise God for the opportunity we have to pray with others who know and love God.
- Ask God for guidance in seeking a prayer partner or a prayer group if you are not in one.
- Pray that our church will be a "house of prayer."

ACTION _____

If you are not involved with a prayer partner or a prayer group, *just do it!*

WEEK 4: Prayer Assignments
DAY 1: *Global Prayer*

MEMORY VERSE _____

"I urge, then, first of all, that requests, prayers, intercession and thanksgiving be made for everyone—for kings and all those in authority, that we may live peaceful and quiet lives in all godliness and holiness."
1 TIMOTHY 2:1–2

Recently, I was challenged by this quote from S.D. Gordon:

The greatest thing anyone can do for God and for man is pray. It is not the only thing. But it is the chief thing....The great people of the earth today are the people who pray. I do not mean those who talk about prayer, nor those who say they believe in prayer, nor yet those who can explain about prayer, but I mean those who *take* time and *pray.*[14]

As we grow deeper in our relationship with Christ and develop a life of prayer, we begin to notice that God places certain situations and people in our minds and hearts with regularity. I call these "prayer assignments." Sometimes these promptings and leanings are a result of our spiritual gifts. For example, if you have the gift of mercy or compassion, you may have a deep desire to pray for the sick and suffering. Our life experiences and our personal interests also give us prayer assignments. Following a trip to Asia, I became more aware of the needs of Christians in China. Now I pray for them regularly, whereas before this trip they weren't even on my radar screen.

This week, we'll focus on five specific areas for prayer. Of course, we could emphasize many more. My desire is that as we go through this week, we will be open to the idea that God has some specific prayer assignments for everyone. I trust that the principles we learn together will be transferable to other assignments not detailed here.

What or who are you prompted to pray for regularly?

First, some general principles regarding any prayer assignment:

- *Pray Faithfully:* When God gives you a prayer assignment, find a way to keep it in a prominent place (photo on your refrigerator door, note on your calendar, etc.) or use "prayer triggers" as a daily reminder to pray.

- *Pray Intelligently:* Learn all you can about the situation or person, so that you can pray with a sense of knowledge and understanding. Read about their projects, study the country, befriend the person in need, keep updated, etc.

- *Pray Specifically:* Pray for specific needs rather than praying generic prayers such as, "God bless their marriage," or, "God be with them."

- *Pray Personally:* Use individual names in prayer rather than praying generally, such as, "God use the missionaries to proclaim the gospel," or, "God give government leaders wisdom in their decisions."

- *Pray Expectantly:* Pray boldly, in faith, believing that God will use your prayers to impact the life or situation with God's power and love. Watch for answers.

- *Pray "Kingdom Prayers":* Seek to pray in line with God's will, using scripture as a guide, as opposed to our typical short-sighted prayers. An example of this might be that we pray for God to build the Lord's character in the person who is struggling as opposed to asking God to relieve the person's unhappy situation.

Today's prayer assignment focuses on "Global Prayer." We start here because our tendency is to pray mostly for the people and situations that we deal with on a daily basis. It is important to realize that God is the God of the whole world, and his power and strength are needed around the world, not just in our sphere of influence.

As we pray globally, we may choose a particular region of the world for which to pray, or we can focus on themes—for example: families, injustice, deliverance from sin, leaders, revival, evangelization, healing, poverty, peace, etc.

Notice from these verses in the Bible how we can seek God for our world. Match the verse with the theme by drawing a line connecting the verse and the theme it expresses.

Psalm 85:6–9	Restoration of families
Psalm 107:4–9	Revival
Psalm 113:5–9	Deliverance from sin
Psalm 138:4–5	Repentance
Isaiah 58:6–10	Rescue of the hungry/poor
Micah 4:3	Help for the poor
Malachi 4:6	Breaking injustice/oppression
Matthew 28:18–20	Blessing on leaders
Acts 4:30	Evangelization
2 Timothy 2:25–26	Peace
Hebrews 8:11–12	Healing

PRAY

- Praise God who is Lord of the nations!
- Confess your apathy about needs around the world.
- Pray for people during and in the aftermath of disasters.
- Pray for 130 million children who lack access to education worldwide.
- Pray that the Bible will be translated for the 3,000 people groups without scripture in their language.
- Pray for God to raise up translators and provide training for them.
- Pray about the great inequities that leave many people hungry and homeless.
- Pray for the peace of Christ to change the way cities and nations are governed.

ACTION

Choose a country or people group. Learn about their government, religions, social problems, and other issues so that you can focus your prayers on them this week. Find out if there is a tangible need that you can meet as well.

WEEK 4: Prayer Assignments
DAY 2: *Prayer for Missionaries & Pastors*

MEMORY VERSE_____

*"I urge, then, first of all, that requests, prayers, intercession and thanksgiving
be made for everyone—for kings and all those in _____, that we
may live peaceful and quiet lives in godliness and holiness."* 1 TIMOTHY 2:1–2

Some of my childhood memories are of having missionary speakers
come to visit our church. Sometimes they would stay in our home. Usually
after we listened to their stories, they would tell us how we could pray for
them and their work. Prayer is a way to participate in the life of missionaries,
whether they are serving nearby or far away. Today, pastors in the U.S.
are much like missionaries. Our country probably has just as many people
hostile to the gospel and to Christianity as do other places around the world.
In fact, I have friends who served as missionaries in Africa, and expressed
that they would never want to trade places with us. They perceive the work
of a U.S. pastor to be more difficult than serving in another country.

Since I was raised in a pastor's family and married a pastor, I am well
aware of the need for prayer support for those involved in ministry. I am
thankful that many people in our churches through the years have taken
on the prayer assignment of praying for us. This is one of the joys and
blessings of ministry.

The apostle Paul asked his friends in Thessalonica to support his
ministry in prayer. It is the request of every pastor and missionary. Write
it out.

2 Thessalonians 3:1, "Finally, brothers [and sisters], pray for us that

Here are some practical ways we can support missionaries and pastors
in prayer, along with scripture, to "pray into and over" them. Write the key
words from each passage.

Give thanks for their call and gifts for ministry–Colossians 1:3–6

Thank God for their leadership and passion for Christ and the gospel. Praise God for the joys and triumphs they experience in their work.

Pray for their personal holiness and renewal–1 Peter 1:13–16; Isaiah 40:28–31

Pray for a close walk with God, for daily time with the Lord in prayer and study, for fresh outpouring of the Holy Spirit upon their lives.

Pray for spiritual protection–Ephesians 6:10–18

Pray for victory over sin and temptation. Spiritual warfare is real. Those in ministry come under the attack of Satan. Pray that God will shield them from the enemy's influence and deception. Ask for freedom from discouragement and anxiety.

Pray for their personal lives; for their physical health, for healthy marriages, for their families, for financial provision–Philippians 4:19

Pray especially for those serving in areas where good medical treatment is inaccessible, where they are in danger. Also pray for times for them to connect with family far away and for healthy priorities. Some in ministry struggle with day-to-day financial hardship.

Pray for ministry effectiveness–2 Thessalonians 1:11–12; John 15:16

Pray for growing opportunities to reach unbelievers, for wisdom, for bold preaching and teaching, and for a strong vision of the ministry before them. Numerous projects are always underway–church planting, building projects, Bible schools, medical intervention, etc. Pray for workers, materials, supplies, and finances to be provided as needed.

Pray for their working relationships. Disagreements, philosophical differences, cultural misunderstandings, and personality clashes are part of life for those in ministry. The apostle Paul encountered these as well. See Acts 15:36–41. What happened and how was it resolved?

Pray for discernment and for a spirit of harmony and unity to prevail in churches and at mission stations. See Psalm 133:1.

These areas for prayer can apply to anyone in a service-oriented, people-influencing profession, and also to lay leaders in the church. As you determine what your prayer assignment may be, use these guidelines to pray specifically and to pray with a sense of expectancy!

PRAY _____

- Praise God for the privilege of praying for leaders involved in spreading the gospel.
- Ask for a heart to pray regularly for your pastors and others you know in ministry.
- Pray today for your pastor/pastors using the guide above.

ACTION _____

Write a note or send an e-mail of encouragement to a missionary or pastor this week, and let this person know that you are praying for him or her regularly as well.

WEEK 4: Prayer Assignments
DAY 3: *Evangelistic Prayer*

MEMORY VERSE_____

"I urge, then, first of all, that requests, _____, _____ and thanksgiving be made for everyone—for kings and all those in authority, that we may live peaceful and quiet lives in all _____ and _____."
1 TIMOTHY 2:1–2

Remembering that intercession is a love ministry, praying for people who don't know Christ shows our love and concern for them. Prayer makes evangelism exciting. For me, evangelism without prayer is scary, especially since I don't have the spiritual gift of evangelism. Even though not every Christian is an evangelist, we are all witnesses. Undoubtedly, we all know people who have not committed their lives to Christ. We each have an assignment to pray for them. Spirit-led witnessing is made possible through prayer. It is God's desire that all people would come to the Lord. See our memory verse for the week. Also, look at Revelation 5:9, "[A]nd with your blood you purchased men for _____ from every _____ and language and _____ and nation."

Also, read Psalm 22:27, "All the ends of _____ _____will remember and turn to _____ _____, and all the _____ of the _____ will bow down before him."

Throughout church history, before revival or mass conversion experiences, God always gets God's people to pray. Have you ever thought of yourself as being part of a movement of God to bring revival to this world? _____ We can praise God that the Lord will do something consistent with God's character in us and in others, as we pray. We can also be glad that God is able to use us in the chain of bringing someone to faith in Christ. Before we begin to pray for people who don't know Christ, we start by praying for ourselves.

What does Colossians 4:2–6 tell us about preparation for sharing our faith?

59

It also seems important to pray for other believers who are sharing their faith. Pray for a good reputation, for courage and strength, and for strategies to reach unevangelized people. We know that many times it takes many contacts, messages, prayers, and conversations with unbelievers before they are ready to make a decision for Christ. Also, pray for other intercessors who, empowered by the Holy Spirit, will pray for your unsaved family members or friends on a regular basis.

Identify three or more people for whom you are praying or with whom you are conversing who do not understand what it means to have a personal relationship with Christ. _____, _____, _____

What kinds of things have you said or done to share your faith?

How have you prayed for them?

Here are some suggestions for evangelistic prayer:

1. Once you are aware of an unbelieving person, talk to God about (*name*) _____ before you talk to (*name*) _____ about God.

2. Read these verses to learn a variety of actions or attitudes God desires for people who are not in a right relationship with Christ. Then pray for what God wants in the person's life depending on his or her particular situation.

   Matthew 13:15

   John 1:12

   John 6:44

   Acts 17:27

   Acts 20:21

   Romans 10:9

2 Corinthians 4:4

Colossians 2:6–7

1 Thessalonians 2:13

2 Timothy 2:22–26

3. Thank God for bringing this person into your life, and trust the Lord to work. Many times, it seems like it takes forever for someone we love to become a Christian. As we pray and share our faith story with someone, we may get discouraged. It really helps to have a few others who will pray along with us. See Hebrews 10:24–25. Link up with two other people and pray regularly for your friends or relatives who don't know Jesus.

4. Claim John 3:16–17 for those who haven't yet accepted him.

5. What about neighbors or casual acquaintances whom we don't know well enough to pray about specifically? As you walk through your neighborhood, place of work, health club, or grocery store, pray that God will use your countenance or speech as a positive witness. Then be ready! What does 1 Peter 3:15 tell us about being prepared?

PRAY _____

- Thank God that the Lord desires that everyone come to faith in Christ.
- Praise God for using you to influence and pray for unbelieving family and friends.
- Ask God to give you insight as to how to pray specifically for those in your sphere of influence who don't know Jesus as Lord.
- Use one or two verses from the exercise above to pray for your unbelieving friend(s).

ACTION _____

Get together with two other friends who are praying for unsaved people and encourage one another to be persistent in prayer.

WEEK 4: Prayer Assignments
DAY 4: *Healing Prayer*

MEMORY VERSE_____

"I urge, then, first of all, that _____, prayers, intercession and thanksgiving be made for _____—for kings and all those in authority, that we may live peaceful and quiet lives in godliness and holiness."
1 TIMOTHY 2:1–2

Prayer for healing is part of the normal Christian life. If you have been involved in a church, you are aware of prayer requests for the sick listed in the Sunday bulletin. This is as it should be, for Jesus and his disciples ministered to the sick throughout their earthly ministry and the church is to carry on this ministry. The church is to be a healing community. Read the following verses and indicate what they teach about healing prayer.

James 5:13–16

Notice the "conditions" regarding healing included in these verses.

Psalm 103:1–5

Notice forgiveness of sin, redemption, love, and compassion are woven with healing.

Psalm 30:1–3

Notice the sense of needing help, and take note of the praise given to God for action from the Lord.

God joyfully uses a variety of ways to bring healing to people. God uses physicians and other health care providers, medicine, counseling, supportive friends, healthy habits—and, of course, God also uses prayer. Healing throughout scripture is likened to wholeness—health of body, soul, and spirit; and, in some texts, the term "to heal" can also mean "to save." Healing is at the very heart of Jesus, whose name literally means "salvation." He is the one who brings wholeness. The ministry of healing prayer brings people to God. Healing is a demonstration of God's love, often inspires deeper devotion to Christ, opens up evangelistic opportunities, leads to richer worship, and deepens understanding of scripture.

Just as Jesus and his disciples brought wholeness to people when they walked the earth, so today we need intervention to provide healing from spiritual sickness (sin, alienation from God), emotional sickness (behavioral turmoil, anxiety), physical illness (disease or accident), relational illness (broken relationships with people), and even at times oppression or possession by demonic spirits.

Read the passages on the chart on page 64 and notice how Jesus healed and what the conditions for healing were. Notice the conversation between Jesus and those he healed or their family members, and note the action/reaction of friends/family. Use the chart to record your observations.

As we pray for sick people, remember what these verses show us. When we pray with and for the sick, it is good to ask, "How can we pray for you?" or, "How should we pray?" After listening to the person in need, listen to the Holy Spirit; and seek God's direction. Pray in confidence, pray in love and compassion, remembering that it is the Lord who does the healing, not us!

Why isn't everyone healed?

Have you ever been asked to pray for healing for someone who was living an unhealthy lifestyle contributing to his or her sickness? How did you handle this situation?

	HOW?	CONDITIONS?	CONVERSATION?	ACTION/REACTION?
Matthew 8:1–4				
Matthew 8:14–15				
Matthew 8:16–17				
Matthew 9:20–22				
Matthew 9:27–31				
Mark 7:32–37				
Mark 8:22–26				
Luke 17:11–19				
Luke 18:35–43				
John 5:2–15				
John 9:1–12				
Matthew 4:23 and 9:35				

PRAY

- Praise God that the Lord heals and saves God's people, even today!
- Pray for wholeness for someone you know who is suffering.

ACTION

Take note of the Sunday bulletin prayer page, and pray a healing prayer for each of those listed.

WEEK 4: Prayer Assignments
DAY 5: *Legacy Prayer*

MEMORY VERSE_____

*"I urge, then, first of all, that requests, prayers, _____ and
_____ be made for everyone—for kings and all those in authority, that
we may live peaceful and quiet lives in all _____ and _____."*
1 TIMOTHY 2:1–2

 As parents, we give great attention to providing for the physical, educational, and emotional development of our children. Perhaps you aren't a parent, but your life intersects with nieces or nephews, neighbor children, or kids in your church. It is wonderful to be around children, and it is good to do all we can to nurture them in every way. As we were raising our two daughters, we were aware that the most important provision we could make was to insure their spiritual prosperity. Now as grandparents, we think about leaving a spiritual inheritance for our family, even more important than leaving a financial inheritance. Just as we make sure daily needs of food, clothing, education, etc., are met, it is even more significant to cover children with prayer for spiritual development and blessing. Prayer not only operates in the material realm, but also in the spiritual realm. Prayer is not limited by time or geography, and often our prayers are more powerful and effective than our presence. The Bible has much to teach us about passing faith along to future generations.

 See what the following verses have to say about a spiritual legacy.

Deuteronomy 6:4–9

Psalm 78:2–7

Psalm 90:1 and 16

Psalm 102:18 and 28

Psalm 145:4

Proverbs 14:26

Proverbs 15:6

Isaiah 44:3–5

Isaiah 59:21

Matthew 6:20

What is the main idea in these verses?

Do you come from a family that left a spiritual legacy for you?

Who left a spiritual trust fund for you?

Are you leaving a trust fund for your family? If so, how?

The spiritual inheritance we leave behind begins with our own personal relationship and faith journey with Christ. As we make God our fortress, the Lord will provide spiritual shelter for future generations. We must make certain that our children know what it means to have a personal relationship with Christ. I had the joy of leading our younger daughter in prayer to ask Jesus to be her Savior when she was in the first grade. Our older daughter made a decision for Christ in Sunday school. Be ready to explain what it means to be a Christian to your family members. God wants to use us to pass along faith to future generations. It's also important that our children hear and see us reading and studying scripture. As Jesus speaks the living Word into us and as God's Word reveals truth and gives guidance, our lives are filled with treasure that we must pass along to future generations. One of my favorite childhood memories is of visiting my great-grandma, who would recite scripture verses to us from John 14:1–4. Great-grandma left a great legacy—I am not afraid of facing death, and never have been, as a result of knowing what God's Word says about heaven. It is great to memorize scripture with children. Their minds are like sponges, and they absorb scripture easily through song or spoken word.

We also leave an inheritance by praying for our children and by teaching them to pray. If you are not in the habit of praying with or for your children daily, start today. It is never too late, and the dividends will be incredible. Just as it is imperative that our children see us reading the Bible, so they will learn from our prayer life.

What are some specific times and ways you can pray with and for children?

How are you teaching your children to pray?

Additionally, as we seek to leave a legacy for our descendants, we seek to avoid the sins of past generations and break strongholds in our families. Many families are plagued with sexual sin, addictive behaviors, negative speech, or the like. Let's break the pattern in our generation. Then, we take opportunities to tell the stories to our children and grandchildren, either in written form or orally, so that they will know the power of God to overcome unhealthy patterns of the past.

Another thing we can leave behind for future generations is a strong church. Jesus calls the church "his body" and makes it clear that we can't reach spiritual maturity outside the body of Christ. As we fellowship with other believers and live in harmony and unity with them, we fill our lives with the beauty of Christ and build a dwelling place for future generations. It's important that we speak well of our church and church leaders, and support it generously with our prayers, time, and spiritual and financial gifts.

How can we pray so our church will be strong for future generations?

PRAY _____

- Praise God for the people who influenced your faith journey.
- Confess any generational sin and turn away from unhealthy patterns.
- Pray for your children and future generations, especially for their spiritual prosperity.

ACTION _____

Tell the story of your family's spiritual heritage to your children or grandchildren today.

Begin writing the outline of the story here.

Week 5: Models of Prayer
Day 1: *Jesus*

"The prayer of a righteous [person] is powerful and effective." JAMES 5:16

You can learn how to pray or to begin to love prayer in many ways. One way is to look at the lives of people who seem to have well-developed prayer lives. Who prays prayers that work? This week, we will look at five biblical characters who model prayer for us. My hope is that as we study their prayers and their prayer life, we will see what powerful, effective prayer looks like and we will love prayer as they did.

As believers in Christ, our lifelong desire is to become more like him. I submit to you that one way to become more like Jesus is to learn to pray as Jesus prayed! No person had ever prayed as Jesus did. E.M. Bounds wrote about Jesus: "Prayer was the secret of his power, the law of his life, the inspiration of his toil, and the source of his wealth, his joy, his communion, and his strength."[15]

Jesus loved to pray. Although his days were packed from morning until night with pressure and responsibilities—teaching crowds, healing the sick, training his disciples, and traveling—he made prayer a top priority. It is rather surprising to consider that prayer was necessary for Jesus, the Son of God. However, prayer was essential for Jesus as he walked around in human form, bombarded by things common to human beings. Although he was God, he was also human. In his humanity, he accepted his need for dependence on God and his need for regular communication with God.

Scripture shows us a lot about Jesus' prayer life.

Notice first that he prayed at every major event in his life. Look up these verses, and write the milestone of Christ's life.

Luke 3:21–23

Luke 6:12–16

Luke 9:28–36

Luke 22:39–44

Luke 23:33–34

Have you made it a habit to pray before major events in your life?

Recall a time when you prayed before entering into a major decision or life event. What was it like for you? Did it make a difference in your attitude toward the decision/event?

As we read through the gospels, we notice that Jesus' prayer life was filled with variety. He prayed at different times and places, alone and with groups, on his knees and with eyes fixed on heaven, in times of sadness and joy, at moments of victory and when in trouble. Match the verses with the corresponding experience or emotion of Jesus by drawing a line from the scripture verse to the when, how, why for Jesus' praying.

Mark 1:35	Time of joy
Luke 5:16	All night long
Luke 6:12	Early in the morning
Luke 10:21	Heart was troubled
Luke 22:41	Prior to performing a miracle
John 6:11	Kneeling down
John 11:41–42	Eyes raised toward heaven
John 12:27–28	Mealtime
John 17:1	Alone

Although the prayer Jesus taught his disciples is referred to as the Lord's Prayer, the prayer recorded for us in John 17 is truly Jesus' prayer. Read John 17, and write some of your observations about for whom and what Christ is praying.

Based on Jesus' prayer, how can we pray for those we love?

Jesus' depth and honesty in prayer is revealed in his prayer of relinquishment in the garden of Gethsemane   recorded in Matthew 26:36–42 and Luke 22:39–44. Richard Foster says, "We do well to meditate often on this unparalleled expression of relinquishment. Here we have the incarnate Son praying through his tears and not receiving what he asks. Jesus knew the burden of unanswered prayer."[16]

Jesus said, "My Father, if it is not possible for this cup to be taken away unless I drink it, may your will be done." (Matthew. 26:42). I think he wondered if there could be any other way for the people to be redeemed, so that he would not have to face a brutal death and separation from God to bear the sins of the whole world. In this prayer, we see the complete surrendering of human will to the will of God: "Not my will but yours be done."

Jesus yielded to God's will, but not without struggle. He sought no quick fix, but rather sweated profusely (Luke 22:44) as he struggled with acceptance of his path. Knowing this about Jesus gives us permission to struggle with God in prayer. We are not locked into a preset, fatalistic future. We work things out with God in prayer, just as Jesus did. Sometimes true dialogue involves real struggle, followed by confident trust in the character of God. God invites us to go deeper with God so we can go higher with God. Just as Gethsemane preceded Christ's finest hour, sometimes our relinquishment leads to an unprecedented fuller, richer, and deeper relationship with God.

Finally, it is good to remember that Jesus' prayer life didn't end when he left the earth, for "[Jesus] is at the right hand of God and is also interceding for us" (Romans 8:34).

PRAY _____

- Praise God for the prayer example Jesus left for us.
- Confess your prayerlessness, and ask God to help you pray more like Jesus did.
- Thank God that Jesus is still praying for us today.

ACTION _____

Perhaps something is plaguing your life—something with which you need to struggle with God in prayer. Don't shy away from it. Courageously pour out your heart to God, just as Christ did in the garden of Gethsemane. Use this page to write the story of this struggle.

Now trust in the character of God to work it out. Pray for courage to relinquish any personal claim and depend on God's will.

Claim Romans 8:26–28.

WEEK 5: Models of Prayer
DAY 2: *Paul*

"The prayer of a _____ _____ *is powerful and effective."* JAMES 5:16

The apostle Paul, the writer of several New Testament books, was known as a scholar of Jewish law. After a dramatic conversion experience, he became a successful church planter and suffered severely for his faith in Christ. Through faith matured by suffering, he became a model or hero of prayer. Scripture prompts us to follow Paul's example. Today, we will focus on several of Paul's prayers. As we do, I'm certain we will grow to love prayer more.

Paul was a man who prayed constantly and taught others to do the same. In his letters, he uses many "time" terms, such as "constantly," "always," "every time," "night and day," to describe his prayers for others. He is a great example of his own teaching to "pray continually."

Look up the following verses to see why Paul was praying constantly, or why he instructed other Christ followers to do the same.

Romans 1:8–10

Romans 12:9–13

Ephesians 1:15–16

Ephesians 6:18

Philippians 4:4–7

Colossians 1:3–9

1 Thessalonians 3:7–10

1 Thessalonians 5:16–18

2 Thessalonians 1:11–12

2 Timothy 1:3–4

What is the common thread throughout these verses?

One reason Paul prayed was to express his gratitude to God for other believers. As much as we like to be thanked, it is also wonderful to have someone thank God for us. That way, God gets the credit deserved and we receive joy.

Is there a person for whom you want to give God thanks today?

Another purpose behind Paul's perpetual praying was that he loved people deeply. Love prompts prayer. Deep love elicits heartfelt prayer. Intercession is a love ministry. However, sometimes our prayers for those we love are very shortsighted. We pray for things such as a good day, good jobs, good health, and happiness. Notice the things Paul prays for on behalf of those for which he sincerely cares (Philippians 1:7–8). Paul knew that his prayers would make a difference in the lives of those in his churches, his "spiritual sons and daughters." Note what he prays about in these beautiful examples:

2 Corinthians 13:5–9

Ephesians 1:17–19a

Ephesians 3:14–21

Philippians 1:9–11

Colossians 1:9–12

1 Thessalonians 3:12-13

After reading Paul's prayers, what impresses you most about his prayers?

How can you revise the way you are praying for your loved ones?

Paul was also aware of his need for the prayer support of others. He wrote in Romans 15:30, "Join me in my struggle by praying to God for me." In Ephesians 6:19 he wrote, "Pray also for me, that whenever I open my mouth, words may be given me." In Philippians 1:19, he assured his supporters, "I know that through your prayers and the help given by the Spirit of Jesus Christ, what has happened to me will turn out for my deliverance." In Colossians 4:2-4, he showed his reliance on the prayers of God's people as he ministers, saying, "Devote yourselves to prayer, being watchful and thankful. And pray for us, too, that God may open a door for our message, so that we may proclaim the mystery of Christ, for which I am in chains. Pray that I may proclaim it clearly, as I should."

Sometimes we are hesitant to ask others to pray for us. Paul's model clearly encourages us to ask other believers for specific prayer support.

Do you have someone regularly praying for you?

If not, whom can you ask to be a regular intercessor for you?

PRAY _____

- Tell God about the specific things you are grateful for regarding members of your family, your church, and your friends.
- Ask God for a heart to pray constantly.

ACTION _____

If you don't have anyone who regularly prays for you, ask someone today.

WEEK 5: Models of Prayer
DAY 3: *Elijah*

MEMORY VERSE_____

"The prayer of a righteous person is _____ and _____."
JAMES 5:16

James 5:17–18 tells us that Elijah was a person just like us. This is an important statement of truth, because usually when we read about prophets such as Elijah, we think they are in a class of their own. We doubt having much in common with people such as Elijah. Today, as we study Elijah, we will not only learn about his powerful prayers, but, more importantly, we will be reminded that the power of prayer is not in the person praying nor the words spoken, but all the power is God's, released through prayer.

What do you know about Elijah?

In James 5:17–18, we learn a few important things about Elijah's effective prayers.

- A righteous person, a forgiven person, has effective prayers. (Have you been forgiven by God when you go to pray?)
- A passionate person, who prays from his or her heart, has effective prayers. (Do you love God so much that you care about what God cares about?)
- A persistent person, who prays continually, has effective prayers. (Do you give up on praying when you hit an obstacle?)

Do you remember a prayer that didn't seem to work?

Looking back over the circumstances, can you see why it may not have been effective?

Elijah had several powerful prayer experiences. Read the texts below and describe the experience.

1 Kings 17:1–6

What was God doing in and for Elijah in Tishbe and in the ravine of Kerith?

During this helpless time in Elijah's life, he was being prepared to be dependent on God. He was alone, away from his family and support system. Elijah would need the resources of God as he faced future challenges. In Jill Briscoe's book about Elijah, *Prayer That Works,* Briscoe writes, "Ole Hallesby says that the basis for all prayer is helplessness."[17] Have you experienced a time of being alone or isolated and wondered what God was up to?

1 Kings 17:7–24

Describe how God used Elijah and his prayer in this scenario.

Briscoe writes, "I wonder if Elijah would have ever moved on if God hadn't allowed the river to dry up?"[18] God sent Elijah to Jezebel's hometown, where he met a very unlikely woman. God took him from a safe environment to the home of an unbelieving family, where together they all learned to depend on God for daily provision. While he was there doing boring work, God was preparing Elijah and the family for upcoming trouble. Notice the importance of relationship development before praying honest, bold prayer. Notice the "whys" spoken aloud. "Tough things must not keep us from praying, but must drive us to prayer."[19] Preparation and passion seem to be part of this effective prayer. Do you know any mother or father with a child in trouble? If you thought God was telling you to say, "Give me your child," and then to ask the Lord to restore healthy, full life to that child, could you do it? Sometimes God trusts us with the privilege of praying "up close and personal," just like Elijah.

1 Kings 18:16–39

This is quite an amazing story. Please take note of the rebuilding of the altar. What is the significance of this?

Look at Elijah's prayer in verses 36–37. When we come to a place of surrender, do we know what to say? Elijah gives a great model. He prayed in the name of the one true God. This gave him great boldness. "Answer me, O LORD, answer me" (v. 37a) shows that Elijah had a grasp on the promise of God to pray in faith. However, the most important aspect of this prayer is that Elijah was most interested in God's heart, and that others would understand and know God's heart. When we pray in faith about putting things in place spiritually, we can pray in boldness. This is when we experience effective prayer.

1 Kings 18:41–46

Considering that Elijah had just had a challenging, though victorious, day, we might expect him to take some time off. Instead, he got back to work, back to listening to the sound of God's activity. This is the place where Elijah got his nickname, "Rain Man." Following the showdown on Mount Carmel, Elijah returned to the mountain to pray. How many times did Elijah pray for rain and send the servant to look for it? _____
At first, the sound of the rain was only audible to God and Elijah. I want to be tuned into hearing what God hears, don't you? Remember, Elijah was a person just like us, and God is still releasing blessing on people today.

1 Kings 19

Since Elijah was a person just like us, he experienced highs and lows. Although he was a man of faith, he also experienced fear and depression. This passage is just as important for us, as we study Elijah's model, as chapter 18. Take note of Elijah's honesty with God. Although he had seen things so clearly just a short time before, now things seemed uncertain and fuzzy. He was experiencing serious burnout. In the midst of the burnout, he kept on talking and listening to God. Our tendency is to take a break from prayer when we grow tired or have doubts about God. We learn from Elijah's experience that God refreshes, renews, and restores his children when they are weary and run to God.
How did God renew Elijah?

How has God refreshed you?

   If you are tired or doubtful, stay under the "broom tree" long enough for God to nourish and restore you. That brings us back to realizing that the basis for effective prayer is helplessness. Elijah came full circle, and so can we.

PRAY

- Praise God for listening and answering prayers of ordinary people like you.
- Remember your past experiences with God, and praise God for the work done in you.
- Pray for endurance to keep on praying for a difficult situation in your life.
- Pray for openness to keep looking and listening for God's activity.
- Praise God for the reward of answered prayer.

ACTION

Do you know anyone under the "broom tree" who needs your help? Make a list of practical things you could do to help. Then take action.

WEEK 5: Models of Prayer
DAY 4: *David*

MEMORY VERSE _____

*"The _____ of a _____ person is powerful and
_____."* JAMES 5:16

David–the shepherd, king, and psalm writer–was a hero of prayer. David was a complex man. He was a passionate musician, tender and sensitive, as well as a strong, brave warrior. He was both righteous and wicked. Let's study some of his background. Match the scripture with a characteristic or action of David by drawing a line connecting the scripture passage and the statement about David.

1 Samuel 13:14   David becomes father of Solomon

1 Samuel 16:13   David kills Goliath with a stone

1 Samuel 16:18   David is anointed by Samuel

1 Samuel 16:21   David is a special friend to Jonathan

1 Samuel 17:50   David has an affair with Bathsheba

1 Samuel 18:3   David, a mighty warrior, succeeds in battle

1 Samuel 29:5–6   David admits his sin and accepts consequence

2 Samuel 5:4–5   David described as a "man after God's own heart"

2 Samuel 7:13–16   David, a musician, speaks well and is fine-looking

2 Samuel 11:2–5   David is an armor bearer to Saul

2 Samuel 12:13–14   David is king over Judah and Israel

2 Samuel 12:24   David receives a special promise from God

What does the expression "a person after God's own heart" mean to you?

81

Read Proverbs 4:23.

What does this verse tell us regarding our hearts?

Knowing some of David's life is helpful. For the purpose of this study, we are going to focus on the Psalms of David. They are beautiful prayers that help us see why David is known as a "man after God's own heart." The book of Psalms is the prayer book of the Bible. These prayers are wonderful models for us. Today, we'll read several of David's prayers to discover how he expressed his heart to God. As you read his prayers, consider using them as models for situations you are facing.

Psalm 3

David is threatened by enemies. In the midst of this, what does he acknowledge about God?

What personal situation does this remind you of?

Psalm 8

A prayer of praise. What can we praise God for specifically?

Psalm 12

It seems like everyone is telling lies. What does David ask God to do?

Have you ever felt the need to ask God to do this?

Psalm 13

A lament or complaint about a prolonged illness. Notice David's honesty about feeling forgotten, but also the acknowledgment of his trust in God. Have you ever felt forgotten by God?

Psalm 18

A song of praise for deliverance. Notice the adjectives or names he uses to describe God in verses 1-3, 30-36, 46.

These are words frequently used in our hymns and worship songs. We can use songs as prayers, too. Which descriptors are most meaningful to you?

Psalm 23

The Shepherd's Psalm, probably the most familiar of David's prayers, is recited in times of distress, fear, and grief. Think of a time when this psalm brought comfort to you.

Psalms 32 and 51

These are prayers of confession. Notice the honesty with which David admits his sin. When we feel guilt and shame over our sin, our strength is sapped. Our weakness can cause us to confess and repent, thereby opening ourselves up to forgiveness and the great freedom only God can give. The next time you offer a prayer of confession, use one of these psalms. Make David's words your own.

Psalm 86

David is "down in the dumps." His model for us here suggests that we praise and acknowledge God's greatness when we are feeling low. Notice what he asks for in verse 11.

What does that mean?

Psalms 103 and 145

These are prayers of praise, remembering the great work of the Lord. As you read these, recall some of the things God has done for you and praise God.

Psalm 139

This prayer reminds us that God knows every detail of our lives, and God is protecting the Lord's precious creation. Feel the love that God has for you as you bask in the beauty of this psalm. God knows all about you, and loves you deeply.

It's not hard to see why David is a model for us, is it? I hope that his prayers have encouraged you today.

PRAY _____

- Praise God for the prayer book of the Bible, the Psalms.
- Ask God for a heart to pray as David did.

ACTION _____

Write your own psalm of lament, confession, or praise.

WEEK 5: Models of Prayer
DAY 5: *Hannah*

MEMORY VERSE_____

"The prayer _____ _____ _____ person is powerful and _____." JAMES 5:16

Both the Old Testament and the New Testament offer us many wonderful female biblical models. When looking for a model for prayer, Hannah is my favorite. Hannah models life-changing prayer. Her story is found in 1 Samuel 1–2:26. Take time to read it in a few different versions of the Bible, if you have access to various translations.

When we first meet Hannah, she is not content with her life. What is going on in Hannah's life to cause dissatisfaction?

What do you do when you are discouraged with your life?

Do you desire something that you have prayed about for a long time, and yet it is not becoming a reality?

It is easy to become discouraged when it seems as if nothing is happening when we pray, but Hannah gives us some insight regarding how we can approach the seemingly desperate situations we face. I think there are five important things we learn from reading the first chapters of 1 Samuel.

1. Pour out your heart to God.

Remember from our lesson on "petitionary" prayer that God likes us to ask the Lord for what we need. When we tell God our heart's desires, it opens up the opportunity to deepen our relationship with God. Our telling God about our needs is basic throughout our lives, because we are dependent on God.

See Psalms 4:1 and 32:6–7. How is the writer pouring out his heart to God?

2. It is good to be specific when we pray.

Look at Hannah's prayer in 1 Samuel 1:11.

This is a radical prayer, isn't it? It seems a bit like bargaining with God to promise that if God grants a son, Hannah will make sure he becomes a minister. I like the detail of her prayer. We saw the importance of praying specifically in our other models of prayer as well. Notice how God answered her (finally), and see how she followed through. See 1 Samuel 1:20–28. This is a reminder that God can change our life situations through prayer.

3. Persistence is important.

Hannah shows us that it is impossible to pray too much. It is okay to pray for the same thing over and over again. As she prayed, she declared her dependence on God and her hope in God's plan.

Look at Luke 18:1–8. What lesson did Jesus teach the disciples? Verse 1 is the key.

Sometimes when we pray it seems like nothing is happening. In many instances, time is required for maturation and development. Think of the rhythm in nature. A mother bird sits on her eggs until the birds are ready to hatch. A mother waits nine months for a human infant to develop.

No situation about which we pray will ever remain the same. We may not see the change, but God is always at work.

Are you praying with persistence for something that needs time and maturation?

See Jude 1:20–22. What are we to do as we wait for the mercy of the Lord?

4. God is enough.

Look at 1 Samuel 1:18. What does the writer tell us about Hannah's countenance as she left the temple that day?

This appears to be a breakthrough. Hannah came to the place of believing that God was enough for her even if God did not answer her prayer. What an incredible example for us. Our tendency is to whine and complain when God doesn't seem to answer, but Hannah came to a point of hoping in and accepting God's plan for her life. Hannah experienced life-changing prayer that day at the temple. She became *better* rather than *bitter*. God's plan was sufficient for her. Hannah's faith brought honor to God.

5. Recognize God as the giver.

Hannah remembered to give thanks after God answered her prayer. See 1 Samuel 2:1–10 for Hannah's song of praise. When God answers prayer, let's not forget to praise God.

PRAY _____

- Praise God for the privilege of pouring out your heart to God.
- Thank God for always being at work, even when you can't see evidence.
- Confess to times of giving up rather than persisting in prayer.
- Pray in detail about a particular situation, and trust God for the detailed answers.

ACTION _____

Start or continue a prayer journal regarding a particular situation for which you have been praying over a long period of time. Go back periodically to see how God has been working and give thanks.

WEEK 6: Blessings and Benefits
DAY 1: *Friendship with God*

MEMORY VERSE

"Do not be anxious about anything, but in everything by prayer and petition, with thanksgiving, present your requests to God. And the peace of God, which transcends all understanding, will guard your hearts and your minds in Christ Jesus." PHILIPPIANS 4:6–7

If people had told me ten years ago that I would be a "prayer mobilizer," I would not have believed them. I saw myself primarily as a wife, mother, and nurse. I had led many Bible studies, did some teaching for young mother's groups, and had been the key speaker at a few retreats; but I certainly did not see myself as someone who would become a teacher and motivator for praying. It begins first in the heart of God, who draws us into friendship with God. Then, at the Holy Spirit's urging, one responds by simply deciding and desiring to develop a friendship with God through prayer.

How we arrive at that decision is unimportant. It could be crisis, persuasion, or life changes. It really boils down to one decision. Do I want my relationship with God to be the primary love relationship in my life? When this is answered with a resounding *"yes!"* the inevitable happens. A deeper friendship with God occurs because of prayer. That becomes contagious and compelling, for, in the practice of prayer, we are ushered deeper into knowing and loving God. Prayer unleashes love for God that is real and all-consuming. Therefore, imagine my surprise when I stopped to look back over the journey to assess progress and was in awe of the unexpected benefits of prayer.

Jennifer Kennedy Dean writes, "Prayer cannot be summed up in a simple two-part equation: my request + God's answer = prayer. Prayer is a process."[20] It is a relationship, and in the process of relationship development, God does the greatest work. During the process of prayer, God changes our hearts from desiring to have our own way to leaning into the ways of God. Andrew Murray wrote, "At our first entrance into the school of waiting upon God, the heart is chiefly set upon the blessings which we wait for. God graciously uses our need and desire for help to educate us for something higher than we were thinking of. We were seeking gifts; He, the Giver, longs to give Himself."[21]

Read Psalms 42:1–2; 63:1; 73:25–26. What does the psalmist desire most?

Jennifer Kennedy Dean also teaches that God works through the prayer process to lift our desires higher. "We start the process desiring something from Him; we end it desiring only Him."[22] When Jesus, the Prayer Teacher, reveals that there is nothing more to crave but God, we realize that the heart of every prayer is: "More of You, More of You."

In fulfilling that desire, Christ draws us into a deeper, more intimate relationship with himself. What does your prayer life tell you about your friendship with God?

Although prayer is a foundational spiritual exercise and discipline for the Christian, more than that, it is a friendship with God that is characterized by excellent, open, honest communication. Intimacy with God is the most important love relationship in life.

What do these verses teach about the benefits of friendship with God?

Deuteronomy 7:9

Psalm 4:7

Psalm 16:11

Psalm 25:9–10

Psalm 63:7–8

Proverbs 18:24

John 8:32, 36

John 14:27

John 15:13–14

John 15:15

Romans 8:28, 31–35

1 John 4:16–17

As much as I enjoy and appreciate my relationships with my husband, children, grandchildren, other family members, and friends, no relationship brings me more joy than my relationship with God—not that *every* minute I spend with God is great fun, and I'm certainly not living in some mystical place.

Friendship with God develops through every experience, including bitter weeping, screams of frustration, laughing out loud, squeals of excitement, tears of joy, and quiet assurance of his presence. The depth of the relationship grows as I spend time reading, meditating, and studying the Bible—in times of stillness as well as in times of frantic activity. Knowing the truth about God and about myself has brought great freedom into my life. I not only love Jesus, I love getting to love him more. I pray that friendship with God will blossom in your life, too.

List three benefits you have experienced as a result of developing intimacy with God.

1.

2.

3.

PRAY _____

- Praise God for the love and desire the Lord has to have a friendship with you.
- Thank God for the blessings brought into your life.
- Ask God to strengthen your desire for deeper intimacy with the Lord.

ACTION _____

Set aside a block of time to do some relationship/friendship building with God. Then tell a friend about what your friendship with Jesus means to you.

WEEK 6: Blessings and Benefits
DAY 2: *Fuel for Faith*

MEMORY VERSE_____

"Do not be anxious about anything, but in everything _____ _____
and _____ with _____ present your requests to God. And
the peace of God, which _____ all understanding, will guard your
_____ and _____ _____ in Christ Jesus." PHILIPPIANS 4:6–7

Does deep and abiding faith strengthen prayer, or does vital prayer fuel faith? This is an issue I have wrestled with for a long time. I've come to the conclusion that the answer to this nagging question is *"yes!"* I'd like us to consider the relationship between prayer and faith today. As my prayer life matures, so does my faith. Increased faith prompts me to love praying even more.

Allow these writers to stimulate your thinking.

Andrew Murray advises us, "Abide in Him and you shall learn what to so many is a mystery: That the secret of the prayer of faith is the life of faith–the faith that abides in Christ alone."

Jennifer Kennedy Dean challenges us: "Faith is not believing something; faith is believing Someone. Faith is not committing you to an idea, but to a person. Faith is responding to the present tense Voice of the Father. Faith is not knowing how God will bring His will into being; faith is knowing that God will bring His will into being. God's ways are not our ways, but you can be assured of this: He is faithful and trustworthy and your heart can safely rest in Him. Don't focus your faith on an outcome. Instead, focus your faith on God."[23]

"To have faith" Becky Tirabassi says, "is to step in the direction toward what is believed to be the planned course of our lives. It is obeying God in the unseen areas of our lives. And, because it is fueled by God alone, faith cannot develop without prayer and the Word. Faith cannot be mustered up, engineered, or manipulated; it is a response from within us, orchestrated by God. It is the supernatural confidence inspired by a supernatural God."[24]

From Alvin VanderGriend we learn, "Praying in faith is not an inner conviction that God will act according to our desires if only we believe hard enough. He wants us to ask, knowing he is there, claiming what he promises, trusting that he will act in line with his nature and that his purposes will be achieved. That's praying in faith."[25]

"Now faith is being sure of what we hope for and certain of what we do not see." (Hebrews 11:1)

In your experience, has your faith in God prompted you to pray?

Have answered prayers fueled your faith? _____ How?

Write what these Bible passages teach about the relationship between faith and prayer.

Matthew 21:21-22

John 14:12-15

Ephesians 3:12

James 1:5-8

1 John 5:13-15

Read Hebrews 11:1-40.

This passage is known as the Bible's "Hall of Faith." The stories are amazing. These men and women of faith have encouraged Christians throughout the ages.

What did Noah do because of faith?

What was the result?

What happened to Sarah as a result of faith?

What was the outcome?

How about the faith of Moses' parents? Would you be able to do what they did?

And then notice the faith of Moses. What are the highlights of his story?

What kinds of suffering did some endure because of their faith? See Hebrews 11:32–38.

Crucial truth is found in verses 1, 13 and 39. The New Living Translation states it this way. "[Faith] is the confidence that what we hope for will actually happen. It gives us assurance about things we cannot see" (v. 1). "All these people died still believing what God had promised them. They did not receive what was promised, but they saw it all from a distance and welcomed it." (v. 13). "All these people earned a good reputation because of their faith, yet none of them received all that God had promised" (v. 39)

It's interesting to reflect on the fact that the people in the "Hall of Faith" didn't get to see the completed work of God in their lifetime. The great reminder for us is that as we pray and obey God by faith, most of the time we only see a few pieces of the puzzle. God has the puzzle completed, and the few pieces we hold in our hands may not make much sense to us today. It's like trying to figure out what a 1000–piece jigsaw puzzle is going to look like based on a few pieces, without looking at the picture on the box. As we pray, we trust in God's plan, because God has the big picture already taken care of–God designed the puzzle, and that fuels our faith and keeps us on our knees!

How do we come to the place of believing and receiving by faith the promise of Romans 8:28? (Take note of vv. 26–27 for the context of the promise.) Write the promise and then answer the question.

PRAY _____

- Praise God for giving you faith to believe in Jesus for your salvation.
- Praise God for being trustworthy.
- Ask God to increase your faith—your ability to focus on Christ.
- Thank God for being willing to hear and answer prayers you bring in faith.

ACTION _____

Think about something you would like to accomplish that needs praying in faith to fuel it. Imagine Christ as the Master Architect of the project. Make some regular appointments with the Designer in prayer to discover what subsequent acts of obedience on your part will make the project a reality.

Or, begin writing your faith story. As you reflect on how God is putting the puzzle of your life together, it will fuel your faith.

Week 6: Blessings and Benefits
Day 3: *Strength to Stand*

MEMORY VERSE

"Do not be _____ about _____, but in _____ by prayer and petition with thanksgiving, present your requests to God. And the _____ of God, which transcends all understanding, will _____ your hearts and your minds in _____ _____." Philippians 4: 6–8

By this time in the study, you may be wondering why there isn't a lesson on "warfare prayer." I think that virtually all prayer is warfare. We are with Jesus, standing our ground against the enemy, whenever we pray. Warfare should never be our primary focus. Christ is our primary focus! Prayer is the means by which God's power is brought to our defense, so that we can stand against the devil's schemes. Whether we are praying for deliverance from the influence of Satan or praising God, we are praying in the power of Jesus and in the presence of the Holy Spirit. We're trusting in 1 John 4:4, "greater is he that is in you, than he that is in the world" (KJV). The devil tries to keep us from praying because he knows that the power of God, which he can't stand against, is made available through prayer. But Satan lost his rights to presume authority in the life of a Christian at the cross. Christ disarmed the forces of evil. So we need not panic when feeling the enemy attack. Rather, we claim the promises of scripture and cry out to the Lord, who gives us strength to stand firm. If God is for us, who can be against us?

See Colossians 2:13–15. What did God do for us through Christ?

Read 2 Corinthians 10:3–5. What are the weapons we use to fight the enemy characterized by?

I've learned that living a praying life is a battle. Times of discouragement come: times when my actions and speech don't reflect that I have a deep faith, times when I feel like my prayers are hitting the ceiling, and times when I don't think God is paying any attention. God is not absent–not even when we can't sense the Lord's activity. A personal relationship with Christ is not based on feelings. Sometimes the battle for intimacy with God through prayer seems physical, because the obstacles are so human, such as fatigue, depression, bad attitudes, or busyness. At the heart, we are fighting a spiritual battle. Ephesians 6:10–20 gives us strength to stand. Read it and answer these questions.

Why do we need the full armor of God?

What are the pieces of armor needed?

Belt of _____.
Breastplate of _____.
Feet fitted with _____.
Shield of _____ to extinguish _____.
Helmet of _____.
Sword of the Spirit, which is _____.

And what follows immediately after the Sword of the Spirit?

Notice that all weapons are defensive except for two. Which are offensive weapons? _____ and _____.

What makes prayer and the Word so powerful?

Intimacy with God, being filled with prayer and the Word, is what gives us strength to stand!

We have all had our share of trouble in our lifetimes, though my struggles might seem miniscule compared to yours. Our family has dealt with tight finances, untimely death, life-altering health change, divorce, false accusations, unhealthy methods of communicating, and multiple relocations, to name a few. Our human tendency is to want to curl up and hide when we are in trouble. Sometimes we stop praying when life becomes difficult. James 5:13 says we should pray whenever we're in trouble. Trouble is a great growth hormone. It can move us from being spiritual dwarfs to becoming spiritual giants. When trouble comes, don't resist it; let it drive you to your knees. Learn to pray in times of darkness; it's where soul-building work happens.

What do these verses tell us to do in times of trouble?

2 Corinthians 4:16–18

Hebrews 12:1–3

James 5:13

As we seek to live lives filled with purpose and meaning, we learn that we can't be effective on our feet unless we have first been effective on our knees. So when we are facing something that seems impossible for us, the first thing to do is call out to God. Everything God requires of us, the Lord provides for us.

Read 2 Peter 1:3 and reflect on it.

Next, having the help of a friend can be a great source of encouragement. We receive strength to stand by praying with and for each other. The devil is scheming to try to get us to fall, and God provides the prayers of others along with the armor of God to keep us strong. I cannot begin to tell you all of the times God has given strength to stand because of the prayers of other Christians.

Then, remember past experiences. Recalling how God has strengthened us throughout difficulties in our lives builds faith.

Finally, we can use our past struggles to help others who may be dealing with similar situations. We can share how God helped us, read the scriptures that encouraged and built us up, or loan a helpful book.

PRAY _____

- Praise God for giving you strength and provision for everything you need.

- Pray that you will be covered with the full armor of God today.
- Ask for courage to face difficulties.
- Thank God for experiences that have shown God's faithfulness to you.

ACTION

Recall a time when you were deeply troubled and God gave you strength to stand. Share your experience with a friend who is struggling with similar issues.

WEEK 6: Blessings and Benefits
DAY 4: *Trust in God's Timing*

MEMORY VERSE_____

*"_____ _____ be anxious about anything, but in everything by _____
and petition, with thanksgiving, _____ your requests to _____. And the
peace of God, which transcends all _____, will guard your hearts
and your minds in Christ Jesus."* PHILIPPIANS 4:6–7

Have you ever been disappointed in God for not answering your
prayer? Have you ever come to a place in your life where you wondered,
"What's the good of prayer?" Sometimes it seems that God doesn't answer.
We wonder if God is ignoring our prayers even though we have been using
a method that "worked" before. Why is it that sometimes God answers our
prayers, and at other times it appears that God is ignoring us? Does God
always answer prayer? Philip Yancey wrote:

> We may experience times of unusual closeness, when every prayer
> is answered in an obvious way and God seems intimate and caring.
> And we may also experience "fog times," when God stays silent,
> when nothing works according to formula and all the Bible's
> promises seem glaringly false. Fidelity involves learning to trust
> that, out beyond the perimeter of fog, God still reigns and has not
> abandoned us, no matter how it appears.[26]

When we doubt God's response to our prayers, we start to focus on
the tools and ask ourselves questions such as, "Did I pray long enough?
Did I use the right words? Am I not good enough?" When Bible promises
seem unreliable and the outcome to our prayers unpredictable, it is hard
to trust. When questions and doubts crop up, I wonder, have we believed
more in prayer than in God? Have we come to a dismal place because,
instead of viewing prayer as a place to meet with a loving God, we have
misunderstood prayer as a way to get our desires fulfilled? If we pray only
because we want answers, we will eventually get irritated and impatient with
God. When being with God and resting in the Lord's presence becomes
the focus of our prayers, we experience life transformation.

Do you remember a time when you wondered if God was hearing or answering your prayer?

What did you learn about God?

I believe that God always answers prayer. Sometimes God says, "*Yes,*" and other times God says, "*No.*" Occasionally God says, "*Go Slow,*" and quite often God's answer is, "*Grow.*" This teaching has helped me to trust God's timing. I don't always understand the way God answers, but I believe in God's sovereignty, and I trust the Lord to do best.

Think about some of your prayer requests. When did you get an immediate "*Yes*"?

When has God said "*No*" very clearly?

What experience with "*Grow*" or "*Go Slow*" answers have you had?

When our prayer requests don't appear to be answered quickly, we find ourselves in God's waiting room. We ask God questions and listen attentively as we wait. Our waiting is active, rather than passive, as in "waiting on tables." Alertness to possible answers allows time to see things we might otherwise miss. How we wait on God's timing says a lot about the depth of our trust. Daily prayer teaches us to trust in God's timing.

Read the following verses and describe the waiting.

Genesis 15:2–5; 18:10–14

1 Samuel 1:1–20

Psalm 130:5–6

Acts 1:4

Romans 8:18–25

2 Peter 3:8–9

Every believer can tell stories of praying without giving up. Some of us have waited long years for healing, for the right job, to become a parent, or for the salvation of a loved one. Though we may not receive the answer we envisioned, we never stop trusting and expecting God to work. Through waiting on God, having the actual experience of persevering, we develop trust and confidence in God's ability to provide. Patience comes not in the begging, but in the hoping and waiting on the Lord. Our confidence is not in prayer—it is in God. When prayer doesn't seem to work, God is still our God. In the waiting, we learn more about God, more about ourselves, and more about the situation. Nothing we pray about ever remains the same. Everything changes!

Trusting in God's timing includes willingness to be open to a change in our plans. We actually expect less from God than God desires to give. We reduce prayer to an activity that matches our experience rather than looking to God. The period of waiting for the granting of some requests is sometimes rewarded by a far greater gift than that for which we asked.

Read John 11:1–44. What happened as a result of Jesus' delay in answering the sisters' request?

"God has a good, loving, and productive purpose for scheduling waiting periods into the prayer process. When He has called on you to wait, it is because the wait is necessary to the outcome. He is doing something during the waiting period that He could not do without it."[27]

PRAY

- Praise God for always answering prayer.
- Ask God to help you trust in the Lord's timing regarding a situation you are waiting on.
- Pray for a focus on being with God in prayer, rather than always requesting things.

ACTION

Imagine a far greater gift coming from Jesus as you wait for answered prayer. Make a list of some of the "greater gifts." Begin to look for those, rather than the answer you originally hoped for.

WEEK 6: Blessings and Benefits
DAY 5: *Power and Purpose for Living*

Prayer alone has no power, but prayer in relationship with God is powerful. James 5:16 says that God acts powerfully and effectively through our prayers. R.A. Torrey stated, "Prayer is the key that unlocks all the storehouses of God's infinite grace and power. All that God is, and has, is at the disposal of prayer."[28] God uses prayer when political action fails, when education, military might, or planning committees can't accomplish change. God uses prayer to change human hearts. The power of prayer is available to us. The power of prayer has changed me!

How has prayer power changed you?

According to John 14:12–14, what can we expect when we pray in faith?

"God wants to answer prayer in such a way that He will be glorified. He wants our lives to be billboards upon which He can advertise Himself. He wants our lives to be stages upon which He can perform. He wants our lives to be trophy cases in which He can display His mighty deeds."[29]

When my husband and I were facing an empty nest, I began to wonder what my life would be like after our youngest daughter went off to college.

We thoroughly enjoyed raising our two daughters, and my mom role was a primary focus, even though I also worked as an R.N. With an awareness that we would probably live many years without having children in our home on a daily basis, I assumed that God would add new value to my life. So I began to pray about my future. I asked God what the plan was for me so that I'd live out the purpose and plan the Lord designed. It became clear over a period of months that prayer was going to be key. Oswald Chambers' words are now mine: "Prayer does not equip us for greater works—prayer is the greater work."[30] While developing a deeper personal life of prayer, I have become convinced that one of the primary purposes God has for me is to encourage others to consider living a praying life. Remember the adage, "Be careful what you pray for"?

See what these verses say about God's plans and purposes.

Jeremiah 29:11–13

Psalm 25:4–5

Psalm 57:2

Psalm 138:8

Isaiah 46:8–11

Do you have a personal mission statement? A condensed and clear statement of purpose is useful in evaluating activities and plans. See Jesus' mission statement in Luke 19:10.

My personal mission statement says: "I seek to live a life that reflects the love of Christ, to do all I can to assure that my family knows Jesus is Lord, and to spend myself encouraging and teaching others to know the joy found in a deep, abiding relationship with God through prayer."

The only way I've found to live a life of purpose with power is through continual interaction with the Savior. That's one of the many reasons I love to pray. Prayer invites and allows God's presence into all areas of life, beginning with simple daily decisions and culminating with knowing life's purpose. God can fulfill the kingdom purpose through us when we are accessible to the Lord.

Read John 15:4–8. What is the key?

As we are abiding in Christ, whose words shape our desires, we begin to desire what God desires. Then, when we ask for what we desire, we discover our prayers are answered. Prayer becomes much more about relationship than about requests. That's when we know we are living in the vine. Our life and prayers bring glory to God. God empowers us to live out the purpose the Lord has for us.

The call to prayer takes me to people and places I never imagined! Are you willing to open your life to the flow of God's power, knowing that God will likely interrupt your life to fulfill the Lord's purpose and plan for you? If you are, be ready for an exciting life, one that reaches beyond anything you, too, could have ever imagined.

Where might God be calling you to stretch and grow?

"I pray that out of his glorious riches he may strengthen you with power through his Spirit in your inner being, so that Christ may dwell in your hearts through faith. And I pray that you, being rooted and established in love, may have power, together with all the saints, to grasp how wide and long and high and deep is the love of Christ, and to know this love that surpasses knowledge–that you may be filled to the measure of all the fullness of God." (Ephesians 3:16–19)

PRAY _____

- Praise God for the power and plan to guide and govern our world and fulfill God's promises.
- Praise God for the purpose for living the Lord has given, or is giving, to you.
- Confess times when you've failed to tap into God's power to advance God's purposes for you.

- Ask God to continue working in you as you make this journey to a prayerful life.

ACTION

Led by the Holy Spirit, write your personal mission statement. Ask a trusted Christian to hold you accountable to live according to your purpose.

Do you have any additional thoughts about your prayer life with God?

APPENDIX

Helps for Discussion Group Leaders

Congratulations! Thanks for stepping up to serve and lead. As a facilitator for the group discussion component for *Your Journey to a Prayerful Life,* you will have the opportunity and privilege of drawing out stories from the group participants regarding how God is teaching them and transforming them through prayer. This will be an exciting process for you.

As you prepare to lead or facilitate the discussion, here are a few tips to keep in mind.

1. Remember, even if you don't feel qualified to lead, God promises to be with you. You will be blessed as you serve.

2. Before your group meets, spend time in prayerful preparation, asking God to use the material and you to encourage the participants. Be sure you have completed all five daily assignments each week so that you are prepared to facilitate learning.

3. During your first session together, ask the members to make attendance at group meetings a high priority. Suggest that they come prepared each week by completing the five daily assignments at home. As in any group, review the importance of keeping anything shared in the group confidential.

4. You will realize quickly that you do not have enough time to have all give their answers to each question. Feel free to determine ahead of time which questions you believe are most important to discuss, or ask the participants which questions were most challenging or meaningful to them from each day's assignment. Use that as a launching point for conversation. It's important to spend time learning from one another about how the daily "Action" was applied, and what was discovered as a result.

5. When you ask a question, be patient in waiting for answers. Don't let a period of silence bother you. Quiet water often runs deep! After someone responds, affirm that person with a simple, "Thank you," and ask, "How about someone else?" Be sensitive to new people. Watch them blossom as you provide a safe setting for them. Involve quieter participants by asking them to read scripture verses. If there is a "dominator" in the group, speak with this person outside of group

time about being sensitive to giving time for others to talk. Let your group members know how important and valuable they are to you.

6. If your group has only sixty to ninety minutes for group meetings, you will only have time to discuss the daily lessons and pray together. Groups that have a two-hour time block have found it beneficial to include a brief teaching lecture, perhaps twenty minutes in length. This teaching can be based either on one of the daily assignments for the week, going deeper into scripture, or on additional resources that will expand the teaching. Additional teaching may involve a prayer testimony from the leader or from a member of the group. I want to encourage you to tap into the teaching gifts apparent in your group and encourage one another by sharing what God has been doing in your life of prayer.

7. Be sure you allocate time to pray together as a group. I recommend not taking "prayer requests" as part of the group time, but instead use the precious time together to actually pray with and for each other. Encourage audible prayer in groups of three to four people or model/ practice a form of prayer taught in the week's lesson. Use variety in this group prayer time from week to week, such as praying for the person on your right, or taking a name home to pray for in the coming week, or singing your prayers together. God is a creative God, so let God's creativity flow through you!

8. If your group is larger than ten, consider breaking into smaller groups occasionally. A smaller circle gives greater opportunity to talk. Generally, people learn and retain more when they verbalize what they have read. Smaller groups are also helpful during prayer time. You may come together for the additional teaching time or for fellowship.

9. Enjoy the people in your group! Pray for each group member by name throughout the week. If your schedule allows, make an occasional phone call or send a group e-mail to encourage members as they study at home. The relationships developed will be just as significant as the study and learning that takes place. At the end of the study, give God praise for what was experienced together!

Notes

[1]The Mainline Evangelism Project studied congregations in seven denominations over a period of four years: American Baptist Churches USA, Christian Church (Disciples of Christ), Evangelical Lutheran Church in America, Presbyterian Church USA, Reformed Church in America, United Church of Christ, and The United Methodist Church.

[2]O. Hallesby, *Prayer* (London: InterVarsity Press, 1959), 7.

[3]Richard Foster, *Prayer: Finding the Heart's True Home* (New York: HarperOne,1992), 7.

[4]Paul Thigpen, as quoted in Cynthia Heald, *Becoming a Woman of Prayer* (Colorado Springs: NavPress, 1996), 61.

[5]Terry Tekyl, *How to Pray After You've Kicked the Dog* (Muncie, Ind.: Prayer Point Press, 1999), 186–87.

[6]Ibid., 187.

[7]Saint Theresa of Avila, quoted in Alvin VanderGriend, *Love to Pray* (Terre Haute, Ind.: Harvest Prayer Ministries, 2004), 29.

[8]Julian of Norwich, *Prayers Across the Centuries* (Wheaton, Ill.: Harold Shaw, 1993), 80.

[9]Alvin VanderGriend, *Love to Pray* (Eugene, Oreg.: Harvest Prayer Ministries 2004), appendix A.

[10]Lloyd Ogilvie, *Conversation with God* (Eugene, Oreg.: Harvest House Publishers 1993), 50.

[11]Richard Foster, "Growing Edges," *Renovare Perspective* 13, no. 2 (April 2003): 1.

[12]Dallas Willard, *The Spirit of the Disciplines* (San Fraciso: HarperSanFranciso, 1988), 184, 185.

[13]Andrew Murray, *Prayer: A 31-Day Plan to Enrich Your Prayer Life* (Uhrichsville, Ohio: Barbour & Co., n.d.), 10.

[14]S.D. Gordon, *Quiet Talks on Prayer* (Chicago: Fleming H. Revell, 1904), 12.

[15]E.M. Bounds, as quoted in VanderGriend, *Love to Pray,* 68.

[16]Foster, *Prayer: Finding the Heart's True Home,* 49.

[17]Jill Briscoe, *Prayer That Works* (Wheaton, Ill.: Tyndale, 2000), 26.

[18]Ibid., 31.

[19]Ibid., 50.

[20]Jennifer Kennedy Dean, *Live a Praying Life* (Birmingham, Ala.: New Hope, 2003), 78.

[21]Andrew Murray, quoted in ibid., 79.

[22]Ibid., 79–80.

[23]Jennifer Kennedy Dean, "52 Prayer Starters," www.prayinglife.org.

[24]Becky Tirabassi, *Let Prayer Change Your Life* (Nashville: Thomas Nelson Publishers, 2000), 137–38.

[25]VanderGriend, *Love to Pray,* 20.

[26]Philip Yancey, *Disappointment with God* (Grand Rapids, Mich.: Zondervan, 1988), 207.

[27]Dean, "52 Prayer Starters."

[28]R. A. Torrey, *The Power of Prayer and the Prayer of Power* (1924; reprint, New York: Cosimo Classics, 2007), 17.

[29]Dean, "52 Prayer Starters."

[30]Oswald Chambers, *My Utmost for His Highest* (1935 [Dodd, Mead and Company]; reprint, Grand Rapids, Mich.: Discovery House, 1995), Oct. 17 entry.

Bibliography

Briscoe, Jill. *Prayer That Works.* Wheaton, Ill.: Tyndale, 2000.

Chambers, Oswald. *My Utmost for His Highest.* Grand Rapids, Mich.: Discovery House, 1995 (original edition in 1935 by Dodd, Mead and Company).

Dean, Jennifer Kennedy. *Legacy of Prayer.* Birmingham, Ala.: New Hope, 2002.

_____. *Live a Praying Life.* Birmingham, Ala.: New Hope, 2003.

_____. "52 Prayer Starters," www.prayinglife.org.

Foster, Richard. *Prayer: Finding the Heart's True Home.* San Francisco: HarperOne, 1992.

_____. "Growing Edges." *Renovare Perspective* 13, no. 2 (April 2003).

Gordon, S.D. *Quiet Talks on Prayer.* Chicago: Fleming H. Revell, 1904.

Heald, Cynthia. *Becoming a Woman of Prayer.* Colorado Springs: NavPress, 2005.

Henderson, Daniel. *Fresh Encounters.* Colorado Springs: NavPress, 2004.

Johnson, Jan. *Enjoying the Presence of God.* Colorado Springs: NavPress, 1996.

_____. *When the Soul Listens.* Colorado Springs: NavPress, 1999.

Julian of Norwich, *Prayers Across the Centuries.* Wheaton, Ill.: Harold Shaw, 1993.

Lucado, Max. *Experiencing the Heart of Jesus.* Nashville: Thomas Nelson, 2003 (workbook edition).

Moore, Beth. *A Heart Like His.* Nashville: Lifeway Christian Resources, 1996.

_____. *Living Beyond Yourself.* Nashville: Lifeway Christian Resources, 2004.

_____. *Living Free.* Nashville: Lifeway Christian Resources, 2002; (Christian growth study plan edition, 2001).

Ogilvie, Lloyd J. *Conversation with God.* Eugene, Oreg.: Harvest House, 1993.

Sacks, Cheryl. *The Prayer Saturated Church.* Colorado Springs: NavPress, 2004, with audio CD.

Sittser, Jerry. *When God Doesn't Answer Your Prayer.* Grand Rapids, Mich.: Zondervan, 2004.

Tekyl, Terry. *How to Pray After You've Kicked the Dog.* Muncie, Ind.: Prayer Point Press, 1999.

Tirabassi, Becky. *Let Prayer Change Your Life*. Nashville: Thomas Nelson, 1995, (revised edition).

Torrey, R. A., *The Power of Prayer and the Prayer of Power*. New York: Cosimo Classics, 2007.

Towns, Elmer. *Praying the Lord's Prayer for Spiritual Breakthrough*. Ventura, Calif.: Gospel Light Publications, 1997.

VanderGriend, Alvin. *Love to Pray*. Terre Haute, Ind.: Harvest Prayer Ministries, 2004.

Willard, Dallas. *The Spirit of the Disciplines*. San Francisco: HarperSanFancisco, 1988.